Preventing Surprise Attacks

HOOVER STUDIES
IN POLITICS, ECONOMICS,
AND SOCIETY

General Editors:
Peter Berkowitz and Tod Lindberg

Preventing Surprise Attacks

Intelligence Reform in the Wake of 9/11

Richard A. Posner

HOOVER STUDIES
IN POLITICS, ECONOMICS,
AND SOCIETY

Published in cooperation with
HOOVER INSTITUTION
Stanford University • Stanford, California

ROWMAN & LITTLEFIELD PUBLISHERS, INC.
Lanham • Boulder • New York • Toronto • Oxford

ROWMAN & LITTLEFIELD PUBLISHERS, INC.

The Hoover Institution on War, Revolution and Peace,
founded at Stanford University in 1919 by Herbert Hoover,
who went on to become the thirty-first president of
the United States, is an interdisciplinary research center
for advanced study on domestic and international affairs.
The views expressed in its publications are entirely those of
the authors and do not necessarily reflect the views of the staff,
officers, or Board of Overseers of the Hoover Institution.

www.hoover.org

Published in the United States of America
by Rowman & Littlefield Publishers, Inc.
A wholly-owned subsidary of
The Rowman & Littlefield Publishing Group, Inc.
4501 Forbes Boulevard, Suite 200, Lanham, Maryland 20706
www.rowmanlittlefield.com

PO Box 317
Oxford
OX2 9RU, UK

Distributed by National Book Network

First printing 2005
11   10   09   08   07   06   05   9   8   7   6   5   4   3   2   1

Manufactured in the United States of America

British Library Cataloguing in Publication Information Available

Library of Congress Cataloging-in-Publication Data
Posner, Richard A.
    Preventing surprise attacks : intelligence reform in the wake of 9/11 /
Richard A. Posner.
        p.   cm.
    Includes index.
    ISBN 0-7425-4947-X (hardcover : alk. paper)
    1. Intelligence service—United States.   2. Intelligence service—Law and
legislation—United States.   3. National security—United States.   4. National
security—Law and legislation—United States.
JK468.I6 6.P67   2005   2005003574

Printed in the United States of America

⊗™ The paper used in this publication meets the minimum requirements
of American National Standard for Information Sciences—Permanence
of Paper for Printed Library Materials, ANSI Z39.48-1992.

Contents

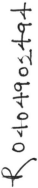

Preface

On July 22, 2004, the National Commission to Study the Terrorist Attacks Upon the United States (the "9/11 Commission") issued the report of its investigation, containing a narrative of the events of September 11, 2001, and their background, and culminating in far-reaching recommendations for reorganizing the intelligence system of the United States in order to reduce the likelihood of future surprise attacks on the nation. On December 6, 2004, four a half months after the issuance of the report, Congress passed, and eleven days later the President signed into law, the Intelligence Reform and Terrorism Prevention Act of 2004, adopting the commission's principal recommendations, although with many additions and modifications.

The rapidity with which the report of an ad hoc committee became a legislative overhaul of a major component of our national security apparatus is a fascinating story in itself, one that I tell briefly in Part I for the weaknesses it exposes in the legislative process and in media coverage of complex issues. But my main concern lies elsewhere—with the soundness of the 9/11 Commission's analysis, the only analysis on which the implementing legislation is based; with the commission's recommendations, so many of which ran the legislative gauntlet successfully; and, of course, with the Intelligence Reform Act itself. The problems with which the commission and Congress wrestled are fundamental, and upon their solution may depend the government's ability to cope effectively with threats to the nation's safety.

A critical analysis of the assumptions that underlie the commission's recommendations and the Intelligence Reform Act may seem of merely academic interest now that the act has been passed. We shall see, however, that the President has great latitude in translating its provisions into concrete rules and practices. The act is just the first stage in the reconstitution of the intelligence structure.

As in most of my previous writing on matters of public policy, I draw on economics (though not to the exclusion of other disciplines)—here regarding a subject to which economic thinking has heretofore made few contributions.

It is a pleasure as well as a duty to acknowledge the help that I have had with this book. I thank Peter Berkowitz for suggesting that I expand the review of the 9/11 Commission's report that I did for the *New York Times* into a book, for his helpful comments on the manuscript, and for guiding the book through the publication process. I also received helpful comments from Luis Garicano, Paul Kozemchak, Tod Lindberg, Kenneth Posner, Raaj Sah, and Geoffrey Stone. Gary Becker gave me useful research pointers, and Lindsey Briggs, Viktoria Lovei, Paul Ma, Meghan Maloney, and Raphael Satter provided exemplary research assistance. John Deutch, Jack Goldsmith, Scott Hemphill, Eli Jacobs, and John Mearsheimer merit particular acknowledgment for their extensive comments on the entire manuscript. I owe very special thanks to Eli Jacobs for arranging meetings with Senator Ted Stevens, FBI Director Robert Mueller, ex–Director of Central Intelligence George Tenet, Jack Downing, John Hamre, Stephen Kappes, A. B. Krongard, John McLaughlin, James Pavitt, and Ted Price, all of whom gave generously of their time to critique my analysis. I emphasize, however, that the views expressed in this book, plus all errors, are my own.

January 24, 2005

Introduction

In the summer of 2004, Sam Tanenhaus, the editor of the *New York Times Book Review*, asked me to review the soon to be issued report[1] of the bipartisan committee known as the 9/11 Commission. The commission had been engaged for 18 months, with substantial staff assistance, in investigating the background and immediate response to the attacks of September 11, 2001,[2] and its report recommended far-reaching changes in the organization of the nation's intelligence system, in the hope of preventing future terrorist attacks within the United States. I had agreed to do the review; despite lacking a background in national security matters, I thought I would be competent to read a document such as the 9/11 Commission's report and identify problems of logic or evidence visible on the

---

1. It was issued on July 22, 2004, as the *Final Report of the National Commission on Terrorist Attacks upon the United States* (2004). See also *The 9/11 Investigations: Staff Reports of the 9/11 Commission, Excerpts from the House-Senate Joint Inquiry Report on 9/11, Testimony from Fourteen Key Witnesses, including Richard Clarke, George Tenet, and Condoleezza Rice* (Steven Strasser, ed., 2004).

2. Richard A. Posner, "The 9/11 Report: A Dissent," *New York Times Book Review*, Aug. 29, 2004, p. 1.

face of the document. I have moreover a fair amount of first-hand knowledge of how government works, and of the likely consequences, therefore, of a government reorganization; I had worked for the Federal Trade Commission, the Department of Justice, and an interagency task force situated in the State Department, in the 1960s, and I have been a federal court of appeals judge for more than 20 years, seven of them as chief judge of my court, where I learned about turf wars at first hand.

Moreover, when I agreed to do the review I had just finished a book on how the nation should deal with catastrophic risks, including the risk of biological and other particularly dreadful forms of terrorism,[3] and the book had addressed psychological and statistical issues similar to those involved in efforts to anticipate surprise attacks. The root challenge facing our security apparatus, moreover, is that of coping with profound uncertainty; and uncertainty is something an American judge confronts constantly because of the unsettled character of American law and the difficulty of extracting truth from the welter of conflicting evidence in a lawsuit. Judges who are self-conscious about their activity know that in the face of profound uncertainty decisions are based not "on the merits" in some abstract sense but on preconceptions shaped by accidents of background and temperament. This turns out, as we shall see, to be at least as true of the evaluation of warning signs by intelligence agencies.

Despite the passage of the Intelligence Reform Act, the 9/11 Commission's investigation and report remain central to the project of reorganizing or "re-architechting" the nation's intelligence system. The report not only laid the factual and analytical foundations of the act; it also proposed many of the structural elements that Congress enacted. It is the natural

3. Richard A. Posner, *Catastrophe: Risk and Response* (2004).

starting point for evaluating the Reform Act and examining the broader issues involved in proposals to reform the intelligence system.

My *New York Times* review commended several aspects of the commission's investigation. The idea of a politically balanced, generously funded committee of experienced people who would investigate the nation's failure to prevent the 9/11 attacks struck me as sound; had the investigation been left to the government, the administration would have concealed its own mistakes and blamed its predecessors.[4] The report itself is a lucid, even riveting, narrative of the attacks, the events leading up to them, and the immediate response to them. The prose is free from bureaucratese, and though there could not have been a single author, the style is uniform; the report is an improbable literary triumph. (It was nominated for a National Book Award.) Particularly notable are the narrative of Osama Bin Laden's career and the rise of al Qaeda, and the descriptions of the confused response by agencies such as the Air Force and the Federal Aviation Administration on the morning of September 11; of the heroic efforts of police and firefighters to rescue the people trapped in the Twin Towers; and of the organization and culture of the various government agencies concerned with intelligence and security matters.

Other features of the commission's undertaking troubled me, however. The delay in the commission's getting up to speed, though apparently not its fault,[5] prevented it from completing its investigation until the Presidential election campaign was well under way. Postponing issuance of its report

4. This is not intended as a criticism of the Bush administration; any administration would have done the same.

5. See, for example, Philip Shenon, "9/11 Commission Could Subpoena Oval Office Files," *New York Times* (late ed.), Oct. 26, 2003, p. 1.

until after the election[6] would have given the commission time to hone its analysis and advice—areas of profound weakness in the report, as we'll see—and politicians wouldn't have been stampeded into a premature, ill-considered commitment to enact the commission's recommendations. One doesn't have to be an expert on national security to realize the absurdity of trying to reorganize a major part of the national-security apparatus of the United States six weeks before a Presidential election expected to pivot on national-security issues, or to recognize the inauthenticity of the endorsement of the 9/11 Commission's recommendations by both Presidential candidates. I am told, however, that the Bush administration would not have granted the commission an extension of time, because it thought it could weather the report better than it could weather the leaks that would have proliferated as the election campaign approached its climax.

On the matter of timing, it is also a shame that the commission could not await the report of the Commission on the Intelligence Capabilities of the United States Regarding Weapons of Mass Destruction. Created by a Presidential executive order on February 6, 2004, and chaired by Judge Laurence Silberman and former Senator Charles Robb, the WMD Commission was assigned to study another recent intelligence failure—the mistaken assessment of Saddam Hussein's program of weapons of mass destruction. (Its report is due March 31, 2005.) The 9/11 Commission did have access to the analysis of that failure by the Senate Select Committee on Intelligence, which issued its report before that of the 9/11 Commission.[7] It

6. The original statute creating the 9/11 Commission directed the commission to submit its final report by May 27, 2004, Public Law 107–306, Nov. 27, 2002, § 610(b), 116 Stat. 2413, but the commission obtained an extension to July 26.

7. U.S. Senate Select Committee on Intelligence, "Report on the U.S. Intel-

is noteworthy in light of the commission's insistence on the need for structural reform that the select committee blamed the Iraq WMD fiasco on poor management and unsound practices of the CIA rather than on the organization of the intelligence system. The committee did suggest that having the same person both run the CIA and chair the system as a whole (before the Intelligence Reform Act, the Director of Central Intelligence doubled as the director of the CIA and as a kind of "chairman of the board" of the entire U.S. intelligence apparatus) gave the CIA disproportionate influence over the formation of the intelligence estimates relating to Iraq's possession of weapons of mass destruction. The problem of undue influence of one agency or official is likely, if anything, to be magnified by the 9/11 Commission's marquee suggestion—the creation of an intelligence "czar"—adopted, though in a diluted form, by the Intelligence Reform Act. An official as powerful as the commission envisaged would exercise greater influence over intelligence estimates than the director of the CIA could ever have done.

The massive public relations effort that the 9/11 Commission orchestrated to win public support for its report before the report could be read invites severe criticism, though the effort was successful: in a poll conducted *before* the report was issued, 61 percent of the respondents said the commission had done a good job.[8] This established a pattern: endorsement of the commission's recommendations, by Presidential candidates, members of Congress, and the press, without critical (often without any) reflection on the soundness of the recom-

---

ligence Community's Prewar Intelligence Assessments on Iraq" (July 7, 2004), at news.findlaw.com/legalnews/lit/iraq/documents.html#script.

8. This figure is from a poll conducted by the Pew Research Center for People and the Press and reported at people-press.org/reports/display.php3 ?ReportID 19; see also www.msnbc.msn.com/id/5456067/.

mendations. The participation of the relatives of the terrorists' victims (described in the report as the commission's "partners")[9] lent a further unserious note to the project, though it contributed to the political momentum of the recommendations. One can feel for the families' loss and understand their indignation at the thought that the deaths might have been prevented, as well as being grateful for their role in urging the investigation, without thinking that the status of being a victim's relative is a qualification for opining on how the victim's death might have been prevented. That is amateurism run wild. And allowing several thousand emotionally traumatized people to drive major public policy in a nation of almost 300 million is a perversion of the democratic process.

Also troublesome, though perhaps inevitable, was the inclusion in the report of recommendations rather than just investigative findings. To combine an investigation of the attacks (the causes, the missed opportunities, and the responses) with recommendations for preventing future attacks is the same mistake as combining intelligence and policy. The means believed available for solving a problem influence how the problem is understood and described. The commission's belief that the intelligence structure should be revamped predisposed it to find that the structure bore responsibility for failing to prevent the 9/11 attacks, whether it did or not. It is true that the statute creating the 9/11 Commission directed it to "investigate and report to the President and Congress on its findings, conclusions, and *recommendations* for corrective measures that can be taken to prevent acts of terrorism."[10] But that needn't have prevented it from concluding that it had no recommendations to offer; and it certainly didn't

9. *Final Report*, note 1 above, at xvii.

10. Public Law 107–306, note 6 above, § 602(5), 116 Stat. 2408 (emphasis added).

require the making of overly ambitious recommendations. A later section of the statute, moreover, requires the commission to submit merely "a final report containing such findings, conclusions, and recommendations for corrective measures as have been agreed to by a majority of Commission members."[11] So a majority of the members could have failed to agree on *any* recommendations without violating their marching orders.

More questionable still was the commissioners' attained goal of producing a unanimous report. Pressure for unanimity encourages just the kind of herd mentality that is being blamed for the other recent intelligence failure that I mentioned—the belief that Saddam Hussein possessed weapons of mass destruction. The achievement of unanimity also distracts attention from the true issues by focusing on the promulgators, viewed as having heroically forged a remarkable consensus.

At least the commission was consistent; its report advocated greater centralization of the government's intelligence activities, and people who prefer centralized, pyramidal governance structures to diversity and competition are often uncomfortable with dissent. But insistence on unanimity, like central planning, deprives decision makers of a full range of alternatives among which to choose. For all one knows, the price of unanimity was adoption of recommendations that were the second choice of members or, as rumor has it, the result of horse trading. The premium on unanimity also undermines the commission's conclusion that everybody in sight was to blame for the failure to prevent the 9/11 attacks. Given the commission's political composition—and it is evident from the questioning of witnesses at the commission's public hearings that none of the members had forgotten which political party he or she belongs to—it could not have achieved unanimity without appearing to

11. Id., § 610(b), 116 Stat. 2413.

apportion equal blame to the Clinton and Bush administrations, and indeed without muffling some of its criticisms, especially of the Presidents and their most senior aides. As a result, while the narrative portion of the commission's report is a great read and contains a great deal of information, most of it probably quite accurate, it is not necessarily a reliable guide to where the principal fault, if there was a fault, in failing to prevent the 9/11 attacks lies.

The mistake in choosing the commission's members was to conflate bipartisan with nonpartisan. The investigation, and report, would have lacked credibility had the commission been partisan, that is, dominated by Republicans or Democrats. But had it been nonpartisan (like Israel's Agranat Commission, discussed in Chapter 3), which is to say composed of people not strongly identified with either party—and there are plenty of those, and many of them are more sensible, fair-minded, and informed than the partisans—it would have told things as they are, rather than blurring the message in the interest of achieving political balance.

As far as the contents of the report were concerned, I was especially troubled by the commission's analysis (as distinct from the narrative portions of the report) and by many of its recommendations, particularly the organizational ones, which occupy only 29 pages of a 567-page report[12] yet became the focus of the congressional and Presidential response. The main organizational recommendation was that Congress create an intelligence "czar," to be called the "National Intelligence Director";[13] a secondary one was to shift the CIA's paramilitary force, called the "Special Activities Division," to the Depart-

12. *Final Report*, note 1 above, at pp. 399–428.

13. The commission's term for what the Intelligence Reform Act renamed the Director of National Intelligence. For simplicity, I shall use the act's terminology even when discussing the commission's report.

ment of Defense; there are others, as we'll see. In light of the fate of czardom, and the increasing use of the term to denote a powerless official, such as the federal drug "czar," the use of the term to denote a national intelligence director is unfortunate, but, in fairness, it was not the commission's term.

The commission's recommendation for centralizing control over intelligence was dubious on its face. The proposal envisaged an organizational nightmare of overlapping authority; and implementation would take years, during which our vulnerability to surprise attacks would be increased as a result of the disorganization, even if only temporary, to which all ambitious reorganizations give rise. Worse, the commission was offering a structural solution to what appeared from its own narrative to be a managerial problem. From the report's description of the failure of the FBI to perform its domestic intelligence tasks competently, one might have inferred that we had too much centralization already, and that it would be sensible to carve out the domestic intelligence function from the bureau and vest it in some counterpart to the United Kingdom's Security Service (MI5), which is a freestanding domestic intelligence agency rather than part of a police force. But that is one organizational suggestion that the commission did not make, or even, it appears, consider seriously.

A majority of the commissioners were lawyers.[14] Their collective background in intelligence was virtually nil and in the administration of large organizations limited, though two were university presidents and two were former governors of major states. None of the members had the stature of Henry Kissinger, originally slated to chair the commission; and a number of other prominent figures more qualified by experience to serve

14. Richard Ben-Veniste, Fred Fielding, Jamie Gorelick, Slade Gorton, Lee Hamilton, and James Thompson. The staff director, Philip Zelikow, also has a law degree.

on the commission than those actually chosen either were not asked or declined, such as Graham Allison, David Boren, Robert Gates, Sam Nunn, William Perry, Warren Rudman, James Schlesinger, Brent Scowcroft, and James Q. Wilson. The report gives no indication that the commission or its staff consulted the relevant scholarly and historical literatures dealing with organization theory in general, with the organization of intelligence in particular, with foreign experience in the organization of intelligence, with the history and anatomy of surprise attacks,[15] with the history of intelligence failures, or with the history of *re*organizations of government agencies—including the very recent history. Thus no critical searchlight was turned on the most closely analogous effort at an organizational solution to the problem of fighting terrorism—the formation of the Department of Homeland Security—despite indications that, if the department has not been an unalloyed disaster, as some believe,[16] it has, at the least, experienced severe birth and growing pains.[17] Another analogous organizational innovation, the creation of the federal drug czar, was also ignored; likewise the evidence that reorganizations proposed by outsiders to the agencies that are to be reorganized cause disorganization in the short run and generally fail to bring about long-term

15. Though there is a paragraph on the Pearl Harbor attack. *Final Report*, note 1 above, at 344.

16. See, for example, Michael Crowley, "Playing Defense: Bush's Disastrous Homeland Security Department," *New Republic*, Mar. 15, 2004, p. 17.

17. See, for example, Robert Block, "Homeland Reaches Juncture: Departures at Agency May Stall Programs or Help Cure Problems," *Wall Street Journal*, Jan. 6, 2004, p. A4; Eli Lehrer, "The Homeland Security Bureaucracy," *Public Interest*, summer 2004, p. 71; Eric Lichtblau and John Schwartz, "Disarray Thwarts Terrorist List, Inquiry Finds," *New York Times* (late ed.), Oct. 2, 2004, p. 12; John Mintz, "Cutbacks Threaten Work of Homeland Security Unit," *Washington Post*, Oct. 31, 2004, p. A6.

improvements, as we'll see in Chapter 5. Nor were other proposals for reorganizing intelligence[18] canvassed.

The commission didn't even acknowledge that its proposal
for a Director of National Intelligence has a history.[19] An executive order of President Carter gave the Director of Central
Intelligence "full and exclusive authority for approval of the
National Foreign Intelligence Program budget submitted to the
President."[20] The experiment was abandoned by Reagan.[21] In
1992, bills introduced by the chairmen of the Senate and House
intelligence committees, David Boren and David McCurdy,
would have created a Director of National Intelligence with
powers similar to those of the DNI proposed by the 9/11 Commission;[22] the bills went nowhere.

Neither was awareness of this history and the relevant
scholarly literature apparent in the hasty consideration of the
commission's proposal of a powerful DNI by Congress and the
Presidential candidates, impelled by political imperatives to
endorse the proposal before they had time to study it. And
where are the media ferrets, the naysayers and skeptics, and
the public intellectuals, when we need them? The media
response to the 9/11 Commission's report was on the whole

18. See, for example, William E. Odom, *Fixing Intelligence: For a More
Secure America* (2003).

19. Russell J. Bruemmer, "Intelligence Community Reorganization: Declin-
ing the Invitation to Struggle," 101 *Yale Law Journal* 867, 886–887 (1992), and
references cited there.

20. Id. at 889, quoting "United States Intelligence Activities," Executive
Order 12036, § 1–602, 43 Fed. Reg. 3674, 3678 (Jan. 24, 1978). See also Peter
Szanton et al., "Intelligence: Seizing the Opportunity," 22 *Foreign Policy* 183,
201–202 (1976).

21. Stephen J. Flanagan, "Managing the Intelligence Community," 10 *International Security* 58, 75–77 (1985).

22. Ernest R. May, "Intelligence: Backing into the Future," in *U.S. Intelligence at the Crossroads* 36 (Roy Godson, Ernest R. May, and Gary Schmitt, eds.,
1995).

uncritical, indeed perfunctory. Reportage and commentary were limited largely to recounting the turf wars and political fights that for a time threatened to thwart the enactment of the commission's recommendations. That those recommendations might be flawed and that the congressional and military critics of the commission might (regardless of their motives) be making valid points failed to register in the journalistic and academic communities.[23]

It is this research and analytic vacuum that I hope to begin to fill in this book. Part I sets the stage. Chapter 1 describes the 9/11 Commission's organizational recommendations against the background of the narrative in the commission's report; I note the disconnect between narrative and recommendations and the shallowness of the latter. Chapter 2 recounts how those recommendations, though plainly flawed, and asserted rather than defended in the commission's report, prevailed in the political marketplace—or at least seemed to prevail, for the legislative response to the report is riven with ambiguities that

23. For exceptions, see Arthur S. Hulnick, "Does the U.S. Intelligence Community Need a DNI?" 17 *International Journal of Intelligence and Counter-Intelligence* 710 (2004); Reuel Marc Gerecht, "Not Worth a Blue Ribbon," *AEI Online*, Aug. 1, 2004, at www.aei.org/publications/pubID.21048/pub_detail.asp; John Hamre, "A Better Way to Improve Intelligence: The National Director Should Oversee Only the Agencies That Gather Data," *Washington Post*, Aug. 9, 2004, p. A15; Anthony H. Cordesman, "The 9/11 Commission Report: Strengths and Weaknesses" (Center for Strategic and International Studies, Aug. 2, 2004); David Boren et al., "Guiding Principles for Intelligence Reform," 150 Cong. Rec. S9428 (Sept. 21, 2004) (the other signatories were Bill Bradley, Frank Carlucci, William Cohen, Robert Gates, John Hamre, Gary Hart, Henry Kissinger, Sam Nunn, Warren Rudman, and George Shultz); and testimony by Henry Kissinger, John Hamre, and others before the Senate Appropriations Committee. *Review of the 9/11 Commission's Intelligence Recommendations: Hearings before the Committee on Appropriations, United States Senate*, 108th Cong., 2d Sess. (S. Hrg. 108–614, Sept. 21–22, 2004). I discuss the media response further in the next chapter, and mention there some exceptions to my negative characterization.

may in the end negate much of what the commission sought to achieve. These two chapters not only identify the most conspicuous weaknesses in the commission's report and the new legislation but also, in conjunction with my analysis in this Introduction of the commission's undertaking, relate those weaknesses to the defective process by which the commission's proposals were formulated, debated, and pushed through Congress.

Part II conducts a more systematic analysis of intelligence reform, drawing on the bodies of thought that should inform responsible reform proposals. It explores themes many of which the reader will have encountered in Part I, but explores them in greater depth. Chapter 3 discusses the history of surprise attacks, seeking a pattern. It focuses on three surprise attacks that turn out to exhibit illuminating parallels to the 9/11 attacks—the Japanese attack on Pearl Harbor in December 1941, the Tet offensive against South Vietnam in the winter of 1968, and the Egyptian-Syrian attack on Israel in October 1973 that launched the Yom Kippur war. It argues, with the aid of a simple formal model, that successful surprise attacks indeed follow a tried-and-true pattern, one that a reorganization of our intelligence system is unlikely to be able to disrupt. Sad to say, to prevent all surprise attacks would be prohibitively costly.

Chapter 4 inquires into the principles underlying the collection and analysis of, and action upon, intelligence, again with the hope of identifying a pattern that can help us think systematically about both means and limits of anticipating and preventing surprise attacks. The focus is thus on the role of intelligence in anticipating such attacks—what is sometimes called "warning intelligence"[24]—although much of my analysis

24. Cynthia M. Grabo, *Anticipating Surprise: Analysis for Strategic Warning* 1–3 (2002).

is applicable to intelligence failure in general. The analysis emphasizes what I call the intrinsic, careerist, and cognitive obstacles, all unlikely to be changed by a reorganization, to constructing a fail-safe system of warning intelligence. I do, however, make several suggestions for modest improvements in the intelligence system.

Chapter 5 conducts a parallel inquiry, this one into the theory of organizations and also of reorganizations, since the commission proposed and Congress decreed a reorganization of the existing intelligence structure rather than the creation of a brand-new one. I argue that theoretical reflection on, as well as experience with, government organizations should make us pessimistic about the likelihood that a reorganization aimed at augmenting centralized control of intelligence will be a success. Coordinating our 15 or so intelligence agencies[25] is vital, but coordination and centralized control are not synonyms. The global economy, a system far more complex than the U.S. intelligence system, is coordinated without any overseer. A modest effort at improving the coordination of intelligence, rejected by the commission and Congress, would have been to separate the positions of Director of Central Intelligence and Director of the CIA and assign the role of coordinator to a DCI who would not be encumbered by having to supervise the day-to-day operations of the CIA. The tighter organization proposed by the 9/11 Commission and endorsed by the Intelligence Reform Act is likely to impede the flow of intelligence data and reduce the diversity of methods and agency cultures that promotes innovative intelligence.

Chapter 6 inquires into the organization of intelligence in other advanced countries that have faced serious internal-

25. Fifteen is the commonest estimate, but because of ambiguities of classification shouldn't be considered exact.

security threats in recent times, notably the United Kingdom in its long-running battle with the Irish Republican Army. We need to understand the experience of nations like the U.K., but also France and Israel, with—what we lack—a domestic intelligence agency. The 9/11 Commission and Congress should have given more consideration than they did to whether to establish such an agency in place of our existing setup, which assigns responsibility for domestic intelligence to the FBI. The pros and cons of such a reform are complex; I argue only that they should be fully ventilated if only because, should there be another major terrorist attack on this country, the pressure to create such an agency may become irresistible. I argue that concerns with the potential adverse impact of such an agency on civil liberties have been exaggerated but in any event should be addressed concretely and empirically rather than just asserted as dogma.

The Conclusion contains some constructive suggestions. The Intelligence Reform Act is now law, and the nation must live with it as best it can till the next legislative overhaul. Fortunately, the process of actually changing the architecture of the nation's intelligence system is just beginning, and ambiguities in which the rushed act abounds create many leeways. I hope that this book will assist thinking about ways in which to exploit these leeways in the national interest.

Part I

___

From the 9/11 Commission's Report to the Intelligence Reform Act

Chapter 1

The Commission's Organizational Recommendations

Between the issuance of the 9/11 Commission's report and the enactment just a few months later of the Intelligence Reform and Terrorism Prevention Act of 2004, based largely on the commission's recommendations, there was no sustained public debate over the merits of the recommendations. They were taken for granted; critics such as Henry Kissinger were ignored. As a result, evaluation of the act must begin with an evaluation of the commission's recommendations, which in turn requires an understanding of how they emerge—or rather fail to emerge—from the report's narrative section.

The commission's tale of how we were surprised by the 9/11 attacks is a product of hindsight; it could not be otherwise. And with the aid of hindsight it is easy to identify missed opportunities to have prevented the attacks, and tempting to leap from that observation to the conclusion that the failure to prevent them was the result not of bad luck, the enemy's skill and ingenuity, the inevitability that some surprise attacks will succeed, the personal failings of individuals,[1] or the difficulty of defending against suicide attacks or protecting a well-nigh infinite range of potential targets, but rather of systemic failures in the nation's intelligence and security apparatus; failures that can be rectified, making us safe, by changing the apparatus.

That's the leap the commission made. It is not sustained by the report's narrative, which actually demonstrates—what is a major theme of this book—the psychological, political, and operational difficulty of taking effective action to prevent a type of attack that hasn't occurred previously and is but one among a large number of possible attacks. Once the 9/11 attacks occurred, measures were taken that have at least postponed a recurrence. Before then, although the government knew that al Qaeda had attacked U.S. facilities (two of our embassies in Africa plus the destroyer *Cole* off the coast of Yemen, and maybe other facilities as well) and would try to do so again, the idea that it would do so by infiltrating operatives into this country to learn to fly commercial aircraft and then crash such aircraft into buildings, killing thousands of Americans in a space of minutes, was so grotesque and so devoid of precedent that anyone who had proposed that we take costly measures to prevent such an event would have been considered a candidate for commitment. There hadn't been even a conventional hijacking of a U.S. airliner anywhere in the world since 1986. Just months before the 9/11 attacks, the director of the Defense Department's Defense Threat Reduction Agency had written: "We have, in fact, solved a terrorist problem in the last twenty-

---

1. As emphasized in Anonymous [Michael Scheuer], "How Not to Catch a Terrorist: A Ten-Step Program from the Files of the U.S. Intelligence Community," *Atlantic Monthly*, Dec. 2004, p. 50. Scheuer, formerly head of the CIA's Bin Laden unit, regards the 9/11 Commission's report as something of a whitewash, contending that senior intelligence and policymaking officials frustrated Scheuer's efforts to come to grips with the Bin Laden menace. I am not in a position to evaluate the accuracy of this charge.

five years. We have solved it so successfully that we have for-gotten about it; and that is a treat. The problem was aircraft highjacking and bombing. We solved that problem. . . . The system is not perfect, but it is good enough. . . . We have pretty much nailed this thing."[2] In such a climate of opinion, not only would efforts to beef up airline security have seemed gratui-tous; they would have been greatly resented because of their costs, including increased airport congestion.

The problem is not only or even mainly that people find it difficult to take seriously risks that have never materialized, that are purely probabilistic (see Chapter 4); it is also that there is no way in which the government can survey the entire range of possible disasters and take costly steps to prevent each and every one of them. As the 9/11 Commission observed with ref-erence to the Federal Aviation Administration—but the point is general—"historically, decisive security action took place only after a disaster had occurred or a specific plot had been dis-covered."[3] The 1993 truck bombing of the World Trade Center led to extensive safety improvements in the Twin Towers that reduced the toll from the 9/11 attacks, but it was only because of that precedent that *any* significant safety improvements were taken in advance of the attacks.

The commission's report states that "the terrorists exploited deep institutional failings within our government."[4] Insofar as the statement refers to a lack of coordination among all the individuals and agencies that could have played a role in preventing or mitigating or responding to the attacks, from

2. Jay Davis, "Epilogue: A Twenty-First Century Terrorism Agenda for the United States," in *The Terrorism Threat and U.S. Government Response: Oper-ational and Organizational Factors* 269, 275 (James M. Smith and William C. Thomas, eds., 2001).

3. *Final Report of the National Commission on Terrorist Attacks upon the United States* 83 (2004).

4. Id. at 265.

immigration officers who check visas to air controllers, it is defensible. But insofar as it refers to the structure of the intelligence system, it is not; or at least it is not substantiated by the report. By 1996, the year the CIA established its Bin Laden station, U.S. intelligence knew that Osama Bin Laden was a dangerous enemy of the United States.[5] President Clinton and his national security adviser, Samuel Berger, became so concerned, especially after the bombings of the U.S. African embassies in 1998, that Clinton, although "warned in the strongest terms" by the Secret Service and the CIA that "visiting Pakistan would risk the President's life,"[6] did visit it (flying in on an unmarked plane, using decoys, and remaining only six hours),[7] and tried unsuccessfully to enlist its cooperation against Bin Laden. A variety of measures were considered for capturing or killing Bin Laden, but none seemed feasible after a cruise-missile attack in 1999 missed him. Invading Afghanistan to prevent future attacks was considered but rejected for diplomatic reasons that President Bush accepted when he took office and that look even stronger after the international political repercussions of our 2003 invasion of Iraq, a species of preventive war. Moreover, it is ungenerous to criticize the government for having been too slow to act on fragmentary information about the threat posed by Bin Laden, when there is a widespread belief that the government acted too hastily in invading Iraq on the basis of fragmentary information concerning the threat posed by Saddam Hussein. That is why it would have been desirable for the 9/11 Commission to await the

5. See also Anonymous [Michael Scheuer], *Through Our Enemies' Eyes: Osama bin Laden, Radical Islam, and the Future of America* (2002).

6. *Final Report*, note 3 above, at 183.

7. Charles Babington and Pamela Constable, "Clinton, Aided by Decoy, Urges Peace on Pakistan," *Washington Post*, Mar. 26, 2000, p. A1. Note, however, the delay between the bombings and the visit.

report of the Robb-Silberman commission (see Introduction) before making far-reaching recommendations for reorganizing the intelligence system.

President Bush's suggestion that his predecessor had merely been "swatting at flies"[8]—the implication being that the new administration was determined from the start to destroy al Qaeda root and branch—is belied by the 9/11 Commission's report. The Clinton administration envisaged a campaign of attrition that would last three to five years, the Bush administration a similar campaign that would last three. With invasion of Afghanistan rejected, nothing good offered. Four years after Bush took office and three years after the United States wrested control of Afghanistan from the Taliban and al Qaeda, Bin Laden remains at large and al Qaeda has not been destroyed, although it has probably been weakened, maybe greatly.

It seems that by the time Bush took office, "Bin Laden fatigue" had set in; no one had feasible suggestions for eliminating or even substantially weakening al Qaeda.[9] The 9/11 Commission's statement that Presidents Clinton and Bush had been offered only a "narrow and unimaginative menu of options for action"[10] is the wisdom of hindsight. The options considered were varied and imaginative. They included enlisting the Afghan Northern Alliance or other potential tribal allies of the United States to help capture or kill Bin Laden, an attack by our Special Operations forces on his compound, killing him by means of a Predator drone aircraft, and coercing or bribing the Taliban to extradite him. But every one of these options proved to be, for political or operational reasons, infeasible.

8. *Final Report*, note 3 above, at 202.
9. Here and elsewhere, like the commission itself, I use "Bin Laden" and "al Qaeda" interchangeably. At this writing, however, Bin Laden's actual role in al Qaeda is unclear and may be small.
10. *Final Report*, note 3 above, at 350.

It thus is not surprising—perhaps not even a fair criticism—
that the new administration treaded water until the 9/11
attacks. But that is what it did. Bush's National Security Adviser,
Condoleezza Rice, "demoted" Richard Clarke, a member of her
staff who was the government's leading Bin Laden hawk and
foremost expert on al Qaeda. It wasn't technically a demotion
but merely a decision to exclude him from attending meetings
of the Cabinet-level "Principals Committee." He took it hard,
however, and requested a transfer from the Bin Laden account
to cyberterrorism. (Clarke, who had met personally with Clinton several times on al Qaeda matters, did not meet with Bush
regarding the al Qaeda menace before 9/11.) Al Qaeda was not
discussed by the Clarke-less Principals Committee until a week
before the 9/11 attacks. The new administration showed little
interest in exploring military options for dealing with al Qaeda.
Secretary of Defense Donald Rumsfeld had not gotten around
to appointing a successor to the Defense Department's chief
counterterrorism official (who had left the government the day
of Bush's inauguration) when the 9/11 attacks occurred.

One reason, not mentioned by the commission (perhaps out
of *politesse*), for the Bush administration's initially tepid
response to the threat posed by al Qaeda may have been that
a new administration is predisposed to reject the priorities set
by its predecessor. Another (though probably minor) reason
may have been the delay in organizing the new administration
that was caused by the litigation, culminating in the Supreme
Court's decision in *Bush v. Gore*, over the outcome of the 2000
Presidential election. Nevertheless these things cannot explain
the administration's lassitude in the face of the anxieties
expressed by George Tenet (the CIA director) and Clarke in
the summer of 2001 over the possibility of an imminent attack
by al Qaeda.

I said in the Introduction that the bipartisan composition of the 9/11 Commission may have caused it to muffle its criticisms of political leaders. Reading between the lines, one senses that the Republican members of the commission thought that Clinton and Berger were aware of the al Qaeda threat but were too reluctant to use force, while the Democratic members thought that Bush, Rice, Cheney, and Rumsfeld were negligent in failing to heed the warnings of Tenet and Clarke. Both criticisms may be merited.

Until the 9/11 Commission's report appeared, the impression was widespread that the failure to prevent the attacks had been due to a failure to integrate (that is, to fit together, as in assembling a crossword puzzle) all the bits of information possessed by different people in our security services, mainly the CIA and FBI, concerning Bin Laden, al Qaeda, and Islamist terrorism generally. And indeed had all these bits been integrated, there would have been a chance of preventing the attacks, but only a chance; the best bits were not obtained until late in August 2001, and it is unlikely that they could have been integrated, understood, and acted on in time to foil the plot. The idea of such attacks was so bizarre that it would have taken unusual imagination to realize what the warning signs added up to.

The narrative portion of the commission's report ends at page 338, and when I first read the report I paused there and asked myself what the results of the commission's investigation implied for how to protect the nation better against international terrorism. The list is short and does not include comprehensive reorganization of the intelligence system:

1. Major buildings should have detailed evacuation plans. Resources for responding to large-scale emergencies should be augmented.

2. Customs officials should be alert for altered travel docu-

ments of Muslims entering the United States; some of the 9/11 hijackers might have been excluded had their travel documents been inspected carefully. Biometric screening should be instituted to facilitate the creation of a comprehensive database of suspicious characters. Incoming freight should be screened. In short, our borders should be made less porous.

3. Airline passengers and baggage should be screened carefully and cockpit doors secured.[11]

4. Legal and, to the extent feasible, bureaucratic barriers to sharing information between the CIA and the FBI, and within the FBI between criminal investigators and intelligence officers, should be eliminated.

5. More Americans should be trained in Arabic, Farsi, Urdu, Pashto, Bahasa Indonesia, and other languages in widespread use in the Muslim world; such training should be a priority for the intelligence services. The commission noted in its report that in a recent year a grand total of six undergraduate degrees in Arabic had been awarded by colleges in the United States.[12]

6. Greater efforts should perhaps be made to penetrate foreign terrorist groups, for example by bribing and black-

11. An attractive suggestion that appears, however, to be infeasible, for reasons well explained in Traci Watson, "U.S. Looks at Which Tech Proposals Will Fly," *USA Today*, Nov. 26, 2001, at www.usatoday.com/tech/news/2001/11/26/tech-proposals.htm, would be to install in every airliner an override mechanism that would enable the plane to be taken over by ground controllers in the event of a hijacking.

12. *Final Report*, note 3 above, at 477 n. 80. The year is not specified, and the figure sounds too low; I have been unable to verify it. A farcical touch is contributed by a recent note that the armed forces have since 1998 fired 20 Arabic linguists because they were homosexual. John Files, "Gay Linguists Dismissed from Military," *New York Times* (Wash. ed.), Jan. 14, 2005, p. A15. One hopes they were promptly hired by the CIA.

mailing members of such groups to "turn" them or even by creating fake extremist organizations to gather intelligence, as in the creation, by Dutch intelligence, of the "Marxist-Leninist Party of the Netherlands."[13] It has been argued that the CIA was mistaken "to deploy the vast majority of case officers overseas under official cover—posing as U.S. diplomats, military officers, and so on" because "there is simply no way that case officers—who still today are overwhelmingly deployed overseas under official cover or, worse, at home in ever-larger task forces—can possibly meet, recruit, or neutralize the most dangerous targets in a sensible, sustainable way."[14] But there are reasons why I introduced this discussion with "perhaps." (1) Life is very dangerous for a U.S. intelligence officer living undercover in a hostile country without diplomatic protection. (2) These officers would stick out like a sore thumb in most African, Middle Eastern, and Western and Southeast Asian societies; it is no surprise that the CIA prefers to employ the local intelligence services ("liaison" services—see next chapter) in these countries. (3) It may not be feasible either to insert undercover agents into al Qaeda or other terrorist groups or to turn existing members. These groups tend to be small, tightly knit, carefully compartmented, fanatical, paranoid, loyal (with their loyalty often cemented by tribal and family ties), and alert. But fringe groups, groups of fellow travelers and sympathizers, may be penetrable and may have useful information.

7. Most, maybe even all, of the thousands of federal agents assigned to the "war on drugs"—a war that is not only

13. Andrew Higgins, "In from the Cold: He Was a Communist for Dutch Intelligence," *Wall Street Journal*, Dec. 3, 2004, p. A1.

14. Reuel Marc Gerecht, "The Sorry State of the CIA," *AEI Online*, July 1, 2004, at www.aei.org/publications/pubID.20911/pub_detail.asp.

unwinnable but probably not worth winning—should be reassigned to the war on international terrorism, where their skills in "stinging" and otherwise detecting and penetrating clandestine organizations and in tracing such organizations' finances could be employed to the greater benefit of the nation. As just explained, it may be unrealistic to expect dramatic results from efforts to penetrate terrorist cells. But there are better prospects for penetrating domestic organizations that provide financial or other assistance to the frontline terrorists, or even furnish recruits.

8. Cooperation among the different agencies, private as well as public, that play a role in preventing or responding to terrorist attacks should be improved. These agencies include building managements, hospitals, police and fire departments, airlines and other transportation companies, U.S. consulates, the Coast Guard, the Federal Aviation Administration, the Centers for Disease Control, the Air Force, and many others, as well as the intelligence agencies.

9. The time may have come to create a separate domestic security agency, on the model of England's MI5, rather than leave sole federal responsibility for domestic security against terrorists and spies to the FBI.[15] In reaction to J. Edgar Hoover's freewheeling ways—and illustrating the tendency of government policy to swing pendulum-like from one extreme to the other (a point to which I return in

15. See, for example, William E. Odom, *Fixing Intelligence: For a More Secure America*, ch. 8 (2003); John Deutch, "Strengthening U.S. Intelligence," testimony before the 9/11 Commission, Oct. 14, 2003, at www.9-11commission.gov/hearings/hearing4/witness_deutch.htm; Paul R. Pillar, "Intelligence," in *Attacking Terrorism: Elements of a Grand Strategy* 115, 133–134 (Audrey Kurth Cronin and James M. Ludes, eds., 2004); William Rosenau and Peter Chalk, "Can We Learn from Others?" *Wall Street Journal*, Apr. 15, 2004, p. A14.

Chapter 6)—the FBI's wings had been clipped; the Supreme Court's expanded conception of the constitutional rights of criminals, criminal suspects, subversives, and radicals was also a factor. Abandoning the penetration and harassment of radical groups, a hallmark of the Hoover era, the Bureau became ever more focused on its core function of investigating federal crimes and providing evidentiary support to federal criminal prosecutions. Increasingly habituated to the leisurely pace of criminal investigations and prosecutions, the Bureau acquired a mind-set reluctant to think in preventive as distinct from prosecutorial terms and predisposed to concentrate its resources on drug and other conventional criminal investigations rather than on domestic intelligence. It became fastidious about the investigative methods it was willing to employ, lest a slip thwart a conviction by tainting some of the evidence gathered in the investigation of the defendant. Its ability to cope with international terrorism was further limited because terrorists have different motivations, goals, and methods from those of the ordinary criminals with whom the Bureau is accustomed to deal, and by the Bureau's traditional reluctance to share information with other agencies lest its criminal investigations be compromised. The flow of information even *within* the Bureau was severely hampered because of the autonomy granted the Bureau's field offices (in part because most crime, even most federal crime, is local) to the point where they became little fiefdoms; and also because the agency proved mysteriously incapable of adopting a modern communications system.[16]

The FBI is an elite police department, with particular dis-

16. See, for example, Anonymous [Michael Scheuer], *Imperial Hubris: Why the West Is Losing the War on Terror* 191 (2004).

tinction in forensic technology, but that is all it is, or at least was at the time of the 9/11 attacks. Of all the agencies involved in intelligence and counterterrorism, it comes off worst in the commission's report.[17] Urged by one of its field offices to apply for a warrant to search the laptop of Zacarias Massaoui (a prospective hijack pilot), FBI headquarters refused because it thought, probably incorrectly, that the special court that passes on requests for foreign intelligence surveillance would decline to issue the warrant. A prescient report on flight training by Muslims in Arizona was ignored by FBI headquarters. Perhaps it is only in hindsight that these seem serious mistakes. Less excusable is the fact that there were only two analysts on the Bin Laden beat in the entire Bureau. Director Louis Freeh's directive that the Bureau focus its efforts on counterterrorism was ignored.

After 9/11, the Bureau, under a new director, Robert Mueller, vowed to do better. His intelligence, commitment, energy, and clarity of aim cannot be doubted. But on whether his efforts[18] will be successful, the jury is still out.[19] It took the

17. For other criticism of the FBI as an antiterrorist agency, see id. at 185–191; U.S. Congress, Senate Select Committee on Intelligence and House Permanent Select Committee on Intelligence, *Joint Inquiry into Intelligence Community Activities before and after the Terrorist Attacks of September 11, 2001* 6, 243–246, 357–359 (Dec. 2002); "Staff Statement No. 9: Law Enforcement, Counterterrorism and Intelligence Collection in the United States prior to 9/11," in *The 9/11 Investigations: Staff Reports of the 9/11 Commission, Excerpts from the House-Senate Joint Inquiry Report on 9/11, Testimony from Fourteen Key Witnesses, including Richard Clarke, George Tenet, and Condoleezza Rice* 239–256 (Steven Strasser, ed., 2004); Odom, note 15 above, ch. 8.

18. Summarized in U.S. Department of Justice, *Federal Bureau of Investigation, The FBI's Counterterrorism Program since September 2001: Report to the National Commission on Terrorist Attacks upon the United States* (Apr. 14, 2004).

19. "Staff Statement No. 12: Reforming Law Enforcement, Counterterrorism, and Intelligence Collection in the United States" (National Commission on Terrorist Attacks Upon the United States, Staff Report, Apr. 14, 2004); "Testi-

Bureau two years after 9/11 just to devise a *plan* to reform its counterterrorism program.[20] Three and a half years after acknowledging in the wake of 9/11 the inadeqacy of its information technology for intelligence purposes and vowing to develop an adequate system, the Bureau still has not succeeded in doing so, despite spending hundreds of millions of dollars, and is not even close to succeeding.[21] It has also been plagued by excessive turnover in the executive ranks of its intelligence and antiterrorism sections.[22] Mueller's efforts to change the culture of the FBI, to the extent that they have succeeded, may prove to have only short-term effects if, as may well be true, there is a fundamental incompatibility between criminal investigations and intelligence operations. Mueller is not a career FBI official, and the career officials may be biding their time until he leaves.

Some of the reforms in my list have been, or are well on the way toward being, adopted and implemented. There have been significant improvements in border control and in aircraft safety. The information "wall" was removed by the USA PATRIOT Act, passed shortly after 9/11. Actually, legislation may have been unnecessary because, as the commission points out, before 9/11 the CIA and the FBI exaggerated the degree to which they were forbidden to share information,[23] and the FBI

---

mony of Dick Thornburgh, Chairman, Academy Panel on FBI Reorganization" (National Academy of Public Administration, June 18, 2003).

20. Laurie E. Ekstrand, "FBI Transformation: FBI Continues to Make Progress in Its Efforts to Transform and Address Priorities" 6 (U.S. General Accounting Office GAO-94-578T, Mar. 23, 2004).

21. Eric Lichtblau, "F.B.I. May Scrap Vital Overhaul for Computers," *New York Times* (late ed.), Jan. 14, 2005, p. A1; Ekstrand, note 20 above, at 13–18.

22. Dan Eggen, "FBI Names 6th Antiterrorism Chief since 9/11," *Washington Post*, Dec. 29, 2004, p. A17.

23. On these misunderstandings, see L. Brett Snider, "Intelligence and Law Enforcement," in *U.S. Intelligence at the Crossroads: Agendas for Reform* 243, 245–248 (Roy Godson, Ernest R. May, and Gary Schmitt, eds., 1995).

exaggerated the degree to which its intelligence officers and its criminal investigators were forbidden to share information with one another. The Bureau was mainly worried about transgressing legal limitations on the disclosure of testimony before grand juries, and the CIA was mainly concerned lest secret information be disclosed in court proceedings. The failure to clarify the limits on sharing was a managerial failure, however, rather than a structural fault.

Efforts are under way to increase the linguistic and cultural competence of our intelligence services. The experience of 9/11 has led to a number of cooperation agreements among various agencies concerned with public safety. And as a result of Director Mueller's vow to refocus the FBI, the Bureau has become somewhat more active in efforts to penetrate extremist groups and has transferred hundreds of agents from the drug war to the war against terrorism. Oddly, one of the simplest reforms on my list—better planning for the evacuation of tall buildings that are attacked—appears to have lagged.

Mention of MI5 under item 9 flags another weakness in the 9/11 Commission's report: American provinciality. Just as our struggle against Islamist terrorism is impeded by our ignorance of the languages, cultures, peoples, politics, and history of the Muslim world, so our ability to devise effective antiterrorist methods suffers from a reluctance to consider foreign models. We shouldn't be too proud to steal good ideas from nations with a longer experience of fighting terrorism than our own. The blows that we have struck against al Qaeda's centralized governance structure may deflect (may already have deflected) Islamist terrorists from spectacular attacks such as those of 9/11 to retail forms such as car and truck bombings, assassinations, and sabotage. Many people in our government believe that al Qaeda is bent on, and will eventually succeed in, launching another major attack in the United States, one that will kill even more people than the 9/11 attacks. If it cannot repeat its success of 9/11, it will lose prestige; if it resorts to the kind of retail terrorism in which Hamas, Hezbollah, and Basque separatists engage in, it will not make the kind of impression on the Muslim world that it wants to. But al Qaeda is not the only Islamist terrorist group, and in time Islamist terrorism may come to resemble more than it does today the forms of terrorism (even if punctuated by occasional attack spectaculars) with which foreign nations such as the United Kingdom and Israel have extensive experience. We should be trying to learn from them. The United States remains readily penetrable by Islamist terrorists who don't even look or sound Middle Eastern; and there are al Qaeda sleeper cells in this country.

Were all the measures that I have listed fully implemented, the probability of another terrorist attack on the scale of 9/11 would be reduced—but perhaps only slightly. The measures adopted already, combined with our operation in Afghanistan, have reduced that probability, and the room for a further reduction may be slight. We and other nations have been victims of surprise attacks before; we will be again. The previous attacks, moreover, as we'll see in Chapter 3, follow a pattern— one that the 9/11 attacks fit to a T and that is exceedingly difficult to disrupt.

Anyone who harbors hopes that the pattern can be disrupted will read with mounting dismay the 90 pages of analysis and recommendations that follow the narrative part of the 9/11 Commission's report. For they come to very little, even though they constitute virtually the entire analytical foundation of the Intelligence Reform and Terrorism Prevention Act. Even the prose sags, as the reader is treated to a barrage of bromides, such as "the American people are entitled to expect their government to do its very best," or "we should reach out, listen to, and work with other countries that can help" and "be generous and caring to our neighbors," or that we should supply the Middle East with "programs to bridge the digital divide and increase Internet access"[24]—the last an unconsciously ironic suggestion, given that encrypted e-mail is an effective medium of clandestine communication. The "hearts and minds" campaign urged by the commission would be no more likely to succeed in the vast Muslim world today than its predecessor was in South Vietnam in the 1960s.

The commission's report urges that criteria be developed for determining which U.S. cities are at greatest risk of terrorist attack, and defensive resources allocated accordingly—this to prevent every city from claiming a proportionately equal share of those resources, when it is apparent that New York and Washington are at greatest risk of being the targets of further attacks. Strict proportionate equality would indeed be arbitrary. But not only is the information lacking that would enable precise allocative criteria to be formulated; in addition, to make Washington and New York impregnable, so that terrorists can blow up Kansas City with impunity, wouldn't do us any good (the psychological impact of striking the American heartland might be even greater than that of another attack on the East Coast). This is one of the abiding problems of preventing surprise attacks: one cannot be strong everywhere, but if resources are therefore so heavily concentrated on the likeliest targets that others are left unprotected, the latter will become inviting targets. This, by the way, is an argument for limiting "profiling": if only people who appear to be of Middle Eastern origin are searched carefully at airports, terrorist groups will focus on recruiting people who do not fit the profile.

24. *Final Report*, note 3 above, at 365, 367, 376, 378.

The commission's report states that the focus of our anti-terrorist strategy should not be "just 'terrorism,' some generic evil. This vagueness blurs the strategy. The catastrophic threat at this moment in history is more specific. It is the threat posed by *Islamist* terrorism."[25] It is certainly *a* catastrophic threat, indeed a threat the commission may have underestimated by failing to focus on the potential deployment by such terrorists of weapons of mass destruction. But is it *the* catastrophic threat? Is it even the *greatest* catastrophic threat? The menace of Bin Laden was not widely recognized until five years before the 9/11 attacks. For all anyone knows, some terrorist threat unrelated to Islam is germinating somewhere in the world—maybe right here at home; remember the Oklahoma City bombers, and the Unabomber, and the anthrax attack of October 2001? Given the breathtakingly rapid advances in the technology of destruction, a threat yet to be discovered may in a few years be actualized as a catastrophic attack greater than anything Islamist terrorism is likely to produce.[26] But if we listen to the 9/11 Commission, we won't be looking out for it because we've been told that at this juncture in our history Islamist terrorism is the thing to worry about.

Illustrating the psychological and political difficulty of taking seriously threats that haven't materialized in the past, the recommendations in the commission's report are oriented toward preventing what is already rather unlikely—a more or less exact repetition of 9/11. Apart from a few sentences on the possibility of nuclear terrorism and of terrorist threats to other modes of transportation besides air, the broader range of potential terrorist threats, notably those of bioterrorism and cyberterrorism, is ignored.

25. Id. at 362 (emphasis in original).
26. Richard A. Posner, *Catastrophe: Risk and Response* 73–86 (2004).

Nevertheless, many of the specific recommendations in the commission's report are sensible, such as that American citizens should be required to carry biometric passports. Other recommendations are in the nature of more of the same—more of the same measures that were implemented in the wake of 9/11 and that have been undergoing refinement, albeit at the usual bureaucratic snail's pace, ever since. One attractive recommendation is to reduce the number of congressional committees, at present in the dozens, that have oversight responsibilities for intelligence. The reason the commission gave for the recommendation was that a reduction in the number of committees would improve oversight; the real reason, probably, was to make it easier for the intelligence "czar" recommended by the commission to control the intelligence system, and this reason rises or falls with that recommendation, discussed next. But actually it's unclear whether consolidating the congressional committees that have fingers in the intelligence pie would increase the powers of the intelligence czar; the committee or committees that emerged from the consolidation (in the limit, a joint Senate-House committee with appropriation as well as authorization power) would be immensely powerful and might see itself or themselves as a peer or peers of the executive branch intelligence chief.

An independent reason for reducing the number of congressional committees with intelligence portfolios is that with so many committees exercising oversight at present, senior intelligence and national security officials spend too much of their time testifying. Another reason is that the more masters one has to answer to, the more the scope for action and initiative is limited because of the differences in their views. Nevertheless both the prospects for such consolidation, given the reluctance of members of Congress to surrender turf, and the benefits are obscure.

An esoteric but nontrivial objection to consolidation has to
do with the large classified portion of the intelligence budget.
At present most of that portion, even if not military, is concealed in the defense budget and thus appropriated by the
defense appropriation subcommittees. The defense budget is
huge, and so provides a nice hiding place. Were the intelligence budget separated from the military budget and made the
responsibility of intelligence committees, both the size of the
overall budget and the appropriations for specific programs
would be more difficult to conceal.

The 9/11 Commission's main proposal—the one the members emphasized in their postpublication campaign to get their
recommendations adopted by Congress, the centerpiece of the
Intelligence Reform Act, and the focus of this book—was to create a new position, that of Director of National Intelligence.
The position of Director of Central Intelligence would be abol-
ished; no longer would a single official both head the CIA and,
in effect, chair the entire intelligence community Instead, the
DNI, shorn of responsibility for running the CIA, would become
not the chairman but the chief executive officer of the intelligence community.

His major assignment would be to overcome the reluctance
of the various intelligence agencies (including the domestic
intelligence branch of the FBI, the State Department's Bureau
of Intelligence and Research, the intelligence staffs in the
Department of Homeland Security, the Federal Aviation
Administration, and other domestic agencies, and the Defense
Department's several intelligence agencies) to share information relating to terrorist activities and to cooperate in other
ways as well in the struggle against international terrorism.
Appointed by the President with Senate confirmation, and
located in the Executive Office of the President with a staff of
several hundred to assist him, he would be responsible for

establishing personnel policies, security policies, and infor-
mation-sharing and information-technology policies for the
various intelligence agencies; would have veto power over the
appointment of the heads of the agencies; and would determine
their budgets.

The sense in which the DNI envisaged by the commission
would have "controlled" the nation's intelligence budget is
complex, however. Congress decides how much money to
appropriate to each federal agency and for which programs of
each agency. The President, through the Office of Management
and Budget, proposes to Congress budgets for the agencies but
his proposals are parceled out to the different congressional
appropriations committees and subcommittees for initial consideration before being voted on by each house. Proposed
budgets for those intelligence services that belong to departments, such as the Defense Department, thus go to the committees responsible for the appropriations for the respective
departments. So while the President can propose a unified
intelligence budget, it is not processed as such by Congress.

To connect the budgetary authority of the Director of
National Intelligence to the proposal to reduce the number of
congressional committees with intelligence responsibilities,
the 9/11 Commission wanted the DNI to be authorized to submit a consolidated intelligence budget for consideration by a
single committee in each house, or perhaps a single committee, a joint committee, in both houses. This would make it more
likely for the administration's budget proposal to be approved
more or less intact, or at least with more or less the same priorities, compared to the existing system in which, for example,
the defense appropriations committees determine the budgets
of the intelligence services in accordance with the committees'
and the Defense Department's priorities.

Enumeration of the specific powers that the commission proposed to vest in a Director of National Intelligence does not convey an adequate sense of his anticipated powers. He was to be more than a supercoordinator of the intelligence services. The report compares him to "a powerful CEO" of a "very large private firm,"[27] describes his role as "managing the whole [intelligence] community,"[28] and declares the goal of the commission's organizational recommendations as a whole to be that of "unifying the intelligence community."[29] The picture is blurred, however, by the commission's adoption, as a model of what should be done with the intelligence services, of the Goldwater-Nichols Department of Defense Reorganization Act of 1986. That act enlarged the powers of the Chairman of the Joint Chiefs of Staff in order to bring about greater unity of the military services.[30] But it didn't make him the CEO of our armed forces. Control of the military remained in the civilian officials of the Department of Defense. If there is a CEO of the armed forces, it is the Secretary of Defense, not the Chairman of the Joint Chiefs. The Director of National Intelligence as envisaged by the commission's report would not have been subordinate to a cabinet member, or to any official other than the President. In effect he would have been the Secretary of Intelligence, though not himself a cabinet member. But he would not have commanded, or appointed the commanders, of particular intelligence operations; and the Secretary of Defense does not share authority over the armed forces with other cabinet officers.[31]

27. *Final Report*, note 3 above, at 414. Or even a "king." Id. at 566 n. 9.
28. Id. at 414.
29. Id. at 399.
30. See, for example, id. at 408–409, 412.
31. Henry Kissinger has made the point succinctly: "Defense must build toward unified action; intelligence should serve coherence in analysis that aids the decision-making ability of senior policymakers." "Prepared Statement of Dr.

So the commission's analogizing of its organizational plan to how the armed forces are structured is flawed. Another reason the Goldwater-Nichols Act is an inapt template for intelligence reform is that Congress in that act was reorganizing a single department and doing so on the basis of studies and debate that had unfolded over years, not months.

The commission's report manages inadvertently to undercut its own proposal for a Director of National Intelligence in a brief section entitled "The Millennium Exception." "In the period between December 1999 and early January 2000," we read, "information about terrorism flowed widely and abundantly."[32] Why? Mainly "because everyone was already on edge with the millennium and possible computer programming glitches ('Y2K')."[33] Well, everyone is now on edge because of 9/11. Indeed, the commission's report identifies no *current* impediments to the flow of information within and among intelligence agencies concerning Islamist terrorism—*the* terrorist threat, according to the report. So sharing is not a problem after all. Yet the principal function of the DNI would be to assure that such information was shared and to prioritize threats—and likewise of the National Counterterrorism Center, the creation of which outside the CIA was another of the commission's recommendations. Ignored was the likely effect on the information flow of the increased complexity of the intelligence system that the creation of the NCTC would bring about. Given the limited number of competent intelligence officers, the short-run effect of creating such an agency would be

---

Henry Kissinger," in Senate Appropriations Committee, *Review of the 9/11 Commission's Intelligence Recommendations: Hearings before the Committee on Appropriations, United States Senate*, 108th Cong., 2d Sess., pp. 5, 7 (S. Hrg. 108–614, Sept. 21–22, 2004).

32. *Final Report*, note 3 above, at 359.

33. Id.

to reduce the number of competent officers in the existing agencies. Likewise with creating a Director of National Intelligence, since the commission wanted him to have a staff of hundreds, doubtless drawn largely from the ranks of existing intelligence officers.

One ought to distrust organizational solutions to managerial problems. There is an illuminating comparison between the 9/11 Commission's report and that of the committee headed by former Secretary of Defense James Schlesinger to investigate the torture of prisoners by U.S. military and contract personnel in Abu Ghraib prison in Iraq.[34] The Schlesinger report explains that the fiasco[35] was the result of specific mistakes in planning, analysis, training, deployment, supervision, and personnel, made by specific individuals whom the report names, up and down the chain of command. There is no finding that the mistakes were the product of, or would have been avoided by, a different structure. For the most part, this seems equally true of the failure to detect and break up al Qaeda's 9/11 plot or at least to respond to the 9/11 attacks promptly and effectively. Inadequate screening of visa applicants, deficiencies in building-evacuation plans, lack of coordination between civil and military aviation authorities, misunderstood rules regarding the sharing of intelligence between criminal investigators and intelligence officers—the list of management failures goes on and on but the only structural failure discernible in the commission's report is the locating of responsibility for domestic intelligence in the FBI, the failure the commission did *not* propose to correct.

34. James R. Schlesinger et al., *Final Report of the Independent Panel to Review Department of Defense Detention Operations* (Aug. 2004).

35. One that brings to mind Talleyrand's quip: it was worse than a sin; it was a blunder. Apparently no useful information was obtained by torturing the prisoners.

The root of failure implied by the commission's report, moreover, was failing to coordinate *all* the agencies, not just the intelligence services, that have a part to play in preventing or responding to terrorist attacks inside the United States (item 8 on my list). In other words, the 9/11 disaster, if indeed it was a "failure" rather than an inevitability (a principal theme of this book is that not all surprise attacks are preventable), was a national failure. So if, as the commission believed, the best way to improve coordination is by centralization, why did it limit its organizational proposals to intelligence? Why didn't it propose a single manager of all public agencies engaged in protecting the United States against terrorists? Did the commission think that improving intelligence is all we need to do to prevent another 9/11? If so, as we'll see in considering in subsequent chapters the systemic limitations of intelligence in detecting impending attacks, it was dangerously mistaken. Or if it held back from proposing an antiterrorist chief because it realized that coordination can often be achieved without centralized control and that centralization can be a source of substantial diseconomies, why didn't it extend those insights to the coordination of the intelligence agencies?

The idea that the reason the bits of information that might with luck have been assembled into a mosaic spelling 9/11 never came together in one place is that no one person is in charge of U.S. intelligence is deeply implausible. How could a high official, far removed from the operating level of the intelligence services, get intelligence officers to share information if they don't want to? Are there no turf wars in the executive branch because one person—the President—is in charge of the whole thing? The reasons for the limited sharing of information within and across intelligence agencies are systemic (see Chapter 4). The volume of information that might contain clues to terrorists' plans or activities is so vast that even with the continued rapid advances in data processing, the relevant data cannot all be collected, stored, retrieved, and analyzed in a single database or even network of linked databases. Legitimate security concerns limit the degree to which confidential information can safely be shared, given nosy media and the ever-present threat of moles like Aldrich Ames and Robert Hansen. And the different intelligence services and the subunits of each service tend, because information is power, to hoard it.

Efforts to centralize the intelligence function are less likely to improve data sharing than to lengthen the time that it takes for intelligence analyses to reach the President, reduce diversity and competition in the gathering and analysis of intelligence data, limit the spectrum of threats given serious consideration, and deprive the President of a range of alternative interpretations of ambiguous and incomplete data to consider—and intelligence data will usually be ambiguous and incomplete. Centralization may lead, moreover, to overconcentration on the single risk believed at any given time to be greatest. An individual's span of attention is limited. The natural bent of a Director of National Intelligence will be to focus on the intelligence problem *du jour*, namely that of Islamist terrorism, to the neglect of other terrorist threats that may prove in time to be as or more serious.

A further reason for questioning the commission's proposal is the heterogeneity of the nation's intelligence services.[36] One of them designs and launches spy satellites (the National Reconnaissance Office) and records visual data collected by them; another uses those data and data generated by other methods of aerial surveillance to make detailed maps of the earth's surface (the National Geospatial-Intelligence Agency);

36. For a good summary, see GlobalSecurity.org, "Intelligence Budget" (Aug. 7, 2004), at www.globalsecurity.org/intell/library/budget/.

another intercepts electronic communications (the National Security Agency); another is the domestic intelligence branch of the FBI; others collect military intelligence concerning state actors such as Iraq, Iran, North Korea, China, and Russia; there are 15 agencies in all. An intelligence czar would find himself in continuous conflict with the Attorney General, the Secretary of Defense, the Chairman of the Joint Chiefs of Staff, the Secretary of Homeland Security, and the President's National Security Adviser. The heterogeneity of the intelligence agencies would defeat his efforts to obtain effective control or even understanding of the entire intelligence apparatus. He would find himself too busy, too distracted by interagency warfare, pulled too hard this way and that, to be able to keep abreast of the latest findings of the intelligence community; and so he would not be able to brief the President adequately.[37] George Tenet, the Iraq WMD fiasco suggests, may have been stretched too thin to be able to give President Bush a properly nuanced briefing. And he had a narrower remit than the Director of National Intelligence is envisaged as having.

In the unwieldy structure proposed by the commission, the DNI would have had veto power over the selection of such civilian and military officials as the head of the FBI's intelligence division and the general heading the armed forces' Special Operations Command. One of the DNI's deputies was to be the Undersecretary of Defense for Intelligence, who would thus have two masters—the DNI and the Secretary of Defense. Tactical military intelligence was to remain in the control of the Defense Department, but there is no bright line between tactical and strategic military intelligence (see Chapter 5).

37. Though why he should be expected to brief the President daily eludes me. Surely there is no exciting intelligence discovery, requiring immediate action, every day.

The DNI's other two deputies were to be the Director of the CIA, who at least would have just one master (but the subordination of the CIA implied by this structure would undoubtedly have adverse effects on the agency's morale), and either the FBI's intelligence chief or the Department of Homeland Security's intelligence chief. The symmetry of the proposal is superficially attractive—the deputies would represent military intelligence, foreign nonmilitary intelligence, and domestic intelligence, respectively. But the commission was not really carving at the joints, because of the overlap among these branches of intelligence. (For example, the CIA does military as well as nonmilitary foreign intelligence.) It was providing a recipe for bureaucratic disaster. Not only would two of the three deputies have two masters, each in a different and rivalrous agency, but the overlap in their duties, as well as the overlap between the DNI's staff and the intelligence agencies, would engender constant interagency strife.

I mentioned the possible adverse effects on the CIA's morale of displacing the agency's director from his central place in the existing structure. This may seem a petty consideration, but it is not, owing to the conditions under which intelligence officers work and the resulting fragility of their morale. As Henry Kissinger explains, "intelligence personnel in the real world are subject to unusual psychological pressures. Separated from their compatriots by security walls, operating in a culture suspicious of even unavoidable secrecy, they are surrounded by an atmosphere of cultural ambiguity. Their unadvertised and unadvertisable successes are taken for granted, while they are blamed for policies that frequently result from strategic rather than intelligence misjudgments."[38] The shaki-

38. Henry Kissinger, "Better Intelligence Reform: Lessons from Four Major Failures," in Senate Appropriations Committee, note 31 above, at pp. 7, 9.

ness of intelligence officers' morale is illustrated by the fact that the appointment of a new CIA director is so often the signal for mass departures by intelligence officers who sense that the new director is not sympathetic to their particular roles or missions.

The commission defended its organizational proposals in part by claiming that our intelligence apparatus was designed for fighting the Cold War and so can't be expected to be adequate to the quite different task of fighting Islamist terrorism. Its report depicts the Cold War as a conventional military face-off between the United States and the Soviet Union and hence a twentieth-century relic (the twenty-first century is to be different, as if the calendar drove history). That is not an accurate description. The Soviet Union fought the United States and its allies mainly through subversion and insurgency, much like al Qaeda. Not that there aren't important differences, not only in motives but in deterrability. Still, it is not obvious, or explained by the commission, why the apparatus developed to deal with communist subversion and penetration should be thought seriously maladapted for dealing with our new enemy. If it is seriously maladapted, we should presumably be looking for guidance to countries that have long histories of fighting terrorism; the commission did not suggest we do that.

The commission's central-planning bent (socialism redux) is further illustrated by its proposal to shift the CIA's paramilitary operations, despite their success in the Afghanistan campaign, to the Defense Department. The report points out that "the CIA has a reputation for agility in operations," whereas the reputation of the military is "for being methodical and cumbersome."[39] Rather than conclude that we are lucky to have both types of fighting capacity, the report disparages "redun-

39. *Final Report*, note 3 above, at 416.

dant, overlapping capabilities" and urges that "the CIA's experts should be integrated into the military's training, exercises, and planning" so that there will be "one fight, one team."[40] A likelier consequence of such integration would be the loss of the "agility in operations" that is the CIA's hallmark. The commission was unaware of the benefits of diversity. The notion that we cannot "afford to build two separate capabilities for carrying out secret military operations"[41] is ridiculous. It is not even a question of building; the United States already has multiple such capabilities—Delta Force, Marine reconnaissance teams, Navy SEALs, Army Rangers—as well as the CIA's Special Activities Division. Diversity of methods, personnel, and organizational culture is a strength in a system of national security; it reduces risk and enhances flexibility. For example, a special advantage of the CIA's paramilitary operation in Afghanistan was that before the operation began, there were already a number of CIA officers and agents there.

The proposal to shift the CIA's small paramilitary capability to the Defense Department underscores the fact that the thrust of the 9/11 Commission's organizational recommendations was to weaken the CIA. The director of the CIA was to lose his position as Director of Central Intelligence. Some of the analytic capacity of the CIA might shift to the DNI's staff. The CIA's Counterterrorism Center was to be largely supplanted by a National Counterterrorism Center outside the CIA. (These are "fusion" centers in which analysts, collectors, and planners of operations join forces to track, and make plans for eliminating, a specific class of enemy threats.) And the CIA was to lose its paramilitary arm. "Central" Intelligence Agency would become a misnomer. To decenter the nation's central intelligence

40. Id.
41. Id. at 415.

agency seems a curious response to an intelligence failure, if that is how 9/11 should be regarded, and a response likely to impair the agency's morale.

What makes such decentering particularly awkward is the CIA's monopoly of clandestine foreign operations, a monopoly that neither the commission nor its congressional followers challenged (though it is now being challenged by the Defense Department).[42] Because of the extreme sensitivity of intelligence data obtained from spies (a leak might easily doom the spy), the CIA's clandestine branch provides its "product"—raw, unevaluated intelligence—only to the agency's analysts, who combine those data with data from other sources, such as signals intercepts, in forming their analyses. The DNI's staff of analysts, if there is such a staff, would not have access to those clandestine data, except at one remove. They would be higher in the bureaucratic pecking order than the CIA's analysts, but have less knowledge on which to base their analyses. This would be a formula for conflict and confusion.

In questioning the centralizing thrust of the 9/11 Commission's recommendations, I do not mean to deny that 15 agencies engaged in intelligence activities require coordination, notably in systems planning and budgetary allocations, to make sure that all bases are covered, to minimize wasteful redundancy (though not all redundancy is wasteful—it builds in a safety factor), and in short to make the many moving parts of a complex machine mesh. Because the Defense Department accounts for more than 80 percent of the nation's overall intelligence budget, the director of the CIA, with its relatively small share (12 percent), could not be expected to control the Defense Department's intelligence expenditures. But to layer

42. Barton Gellman, "Secret Unit Expands Rumsfeld's Domain: New Espionage Branch Delving into CIA Territory," *Washington Post*, Jan. 23, 2005, p. 1A.

another official on top of the CIA director, one who would be in continuous conflict with him, with the Secretary of Defense, and with other officials, is not an obviously correct solution. The commission had no solution.

One can sympathize with the commission's dilemma. To conclude after a protracted and much ballyhooed investigation that there is really rather little that can be done to reduce the likelihood of future terrorist attacks beyond what is being done already—at least if the focus is on the sort of terrorist attacks that have occurred in the past rather than on the newer threats of bioterrorism, nuclear terrorism, and cyberterrorism, about which we may indeed be doing too little—would bespeak a fatalism that goes against the American grain. When an American dies at the age of 95, his family is apt to ascribe his death to a medical failure. (This is what is known in theological circles as the Pelagian heresy—the idea that the human will can conquer all adversities.) In other words, every nonsuccess is deemed a culpable failure. One unfortunate consequence is that the people who get blamed for an undesired outcome are the people who were doing their best—and their best may have been very good—to prevent it from happening. The payment of enormous sums of money to the families of the victims of the 9/11 attacks, as if they were victims of tortious conduct rather than casualties of war, is another symptom of this American cultural peculiarity. Yet how callous it would sound to say to the families of the victims, it was just one of those things. Even in tort law, though, when liability is governed by a negligence standard, a defendant must pay only when a judge or jury determines that he failed to exercise reasonable care; it is understood that some injuries occur without culpability, simply because the costs of preventing the injury would have exceeded the expected benefits. This obvious point was overlooked in the case of the 9/11 attacks. The reason, I think, is that people exaggerate the degree to which it is possible to foresee a surprise attack.

Because of this exaggeration, the instinctive reaction to an attack of the magnitude of the Pearl Harbor or 9/11 attacks is not that we were surprised once again by a clever adversary exploiting the aggressor's inherent advantage of surprise, but that we must have had the wrong strategies or structure and let's change them and then everything will be fine. The victims of 9/11 will not have died in vain. The families' grief will be at least partially assuaged. Actually, I shall argue, the strategies and structure, so far as one can judge, weren't so bad; they've been improved; further improvements will probably have only a marginal effect; and greater dangers may be gathering of which we are unaware and haven't a clue as to how to prevent. A banal point, but one important not to overlook, is that in the three a half years since 9/11 there have been no further terrorist attacks on the United States. Our intelligence system may not be broken after all. It is true that al Qaeda likes to space its spectacular attacks. But since our invasion of Afghanistan after 9/11 it has had compelling incentives to retaliate against us promptly and has repeatedly threatened to do so. We must try not to become complacent, because the threat remains very real. But a top-heavy, Rube Goldberg–style reorganization of the intelligence systerm may well increase rather than reduce the dangers that face us.

Chapter 2

The Congressional Response

Despite their manifold flaws, the organizational recommendations in the 9/11 Commission's report evoked, as we know, a prompt and largely positive congressional response. It is important to trace the path from the commission's report to the final legislative action and see how that action so far altered the commission's recommendations as to leave the issue of the organization of the intelligence system in considerable flux.

One of the first congressional responses was by Senator Pat Roberts.[1] His proposal, intended as an improvement on the commission's proposals, actually highlighted the problems with them. He proposed to break the CIA into three parts (collection, analysis, and science/technology) and also to carve out a new agency from the Defense Intelligence Agency, while placing all the intelligence agencies under a Director of

---

1. 9/11 National Security Protection Act of 2004, at www.fas.org/irp/con gress/2004_cr/roberts-911nspa.pdf (visited on Nov. 5, 2004). For a detailed comparison of his proposal with others that I do not discuss, and with the law existing before the Intelligence Reform Act, see Alfred Cumming, "Comparison of 9/11 Commission Recommended Intelligence Reforms, H.R. 4104, S. 190, S. 1520, S. 6, H.R. 4584, and Current Law" (Congressional Research Service, CRS Report RL32600, Oct. 6, 2004).

National Intelligence. It is unclear what he wanted to do with the intelligence branches of the uniformed military services, so it's unclear just how many intelligence agencies he envisaged the DNI directing. But it could easily be as many as 18, since he planned to add three to the existing 15.

The intelligence agencies, as I have noted, are highly diverse, and like the commission itself Senator Roberts seems not to have considered whether it would make good management sense to place all under a single official. (The idea of fragmenting the CIA is independently objectionable, for reasons that will become clear in subsequent chapters.) There is some optimum span of control, which his proposal if adopted would probably have exceeded. It would be highly unusual in any organization for 18 divisions to report directly to the chief executive, especially if they were as diverse as our intelligence agencies. The agencies should probably be grouped, to reduce the number of officials reporting directly to the chief executive. Well, they are grouped; a number of them are part of the Defense Department. The proposal would have taken them out of the department's control; that seems a mistake, one rectified, however, in the legislation ultimately adopted.

On September 23, 2004—at the height of the Presidential election campaign—Senator Susan Collins introduced a bill (S. 2845) intended to enact the 9/11 Commission's major recommendations. Senator Collins is the chairman of the Governmental Affairs Committee of the Senate, and Senate Majority Leader Frist designated her committee to steer intelligence reform legislation through the Senate, which she did, along with Senator Lieberman, the ranking Democratic member of the committee. Lieberman, along with Senator McCain, had been the prime mover in the creation of the 9/11 Commission, but neither he nor Collins (nor for that matter McCain) are experts in intelligence. The choice of the Governmental Affairs

Committee to shepherd the reform legislation through the Senate was therefore an odd one. There is both a Senate Select Intelligence Committee and a Senate Committee on the Armed Forces, both more experienced in matters relating to intelligence than the Governmental Affairs Committee. By bypassing those committees, which might well have had reservations that would have delayed Senate passage of the Collins bill, the Majority Leader's decision removed a potential obstacle to swift passage. And indeed the Senate passed the bill only two weeks after it had been introduced, by a vote of 96 to 2. That was a true legislative stampede. A different bill, sponsored by the Speaker of the House, passed the House, again in two weeks, on October 8. The bills were referred to a conference committee to iron out the differences between them.

The Senate version stuck pretty closely to the 9/11 Commission's recommendations.[2] Among the principal differences that bear on the structural issues that are my principal concern, the bill eliminated the requirement of "dual-hatted" deputies to the Director of National Intelligence (the Undersecretary of Defense for Intelligence and the intelligence chief either of the FBI or of the Department of Homeland Security); dropped the proposal to transfer the CIA's paramilitary division to the Defense Department; established an Office of Alternative Assessments to serve a "devil's advocate" role in the intelligence community; required every FBI agent to have some training in intelligence (a Band-Aid solution if ever there was one); created a civil liberties watchdog board; but left the existing system of multicommittee congressional oversight intact.

2. For a detailed comparison of the Senate and House bills both with each other and with the 9/11 Commission's proposals, see Alfred Cumming, "Comparison of 9/11 Commission Recommended Intelligence Reforms, S. 2845, S. 2774, H.R. 5024, Administration Proposal, H.R. 10, Current Law" (Congressional Research Service, CRS Report RL32601, Oct. 6, 2004).

The House version (H.R. 10), in response to concerns expressed by defense officials, reduced the DNI's authority, particularly his authority over the Defense Department's intelligence budget. But the main respect in which the House bill differed from the Senate bill was that it added a number of provisions designed to strengthen domestic law enforcement rather than to restructure the intelligence system. Not that the Senate bill was limited to structure. Although that is my emphasis, the 9/11 Commission had made a number of other recommendations and many were included in both bills. But the House bill added provisions that went beyond what either the commission proposed or the Senate included in its bill. Among these were provisions imposing new restrictions on the rights of asylum seekers and other immigrants, such as a ban on issuing drivers' licenses to illegal immigrants and an amendment to the Foreign Intelligence Surveillance Act to enable the bugging and wiretapping of noncitizens even if they aren't suspected of being agents of a foreign power or group, but instead are "lone wolves." Such provisions,[3] while driving a wedge between the Senate and House conferees, are peripheral to my concerns.

Although the 9/11 Commission's organizational recommendations not only were questionable on their face but were barely defended either in the report or in the postpublication television appearances of the commissioners and their allies, the only criticism of the recommendations that received significant public attention during the congressional consideration of the bills came from defense officials and their congressional supporters. The criticism was cast in demagogic terms as a concern that the Director of National Intelligence

3. The lone-wolf amendment survived into the legislation as enacted. Intelligence Reform and Terrorism Prevention Act of 2004, Title VI, § 6001(a), adding 50 U.S.C. § 1801(b)(1)(C). The drivers' license ban did not.

would somehow interfere with the transmission of tactical intelligence from military spy satellites to troops in the field, thus endangering the troops. This concern was parried by adding a provision retaining the Defense Department's monopoly of tactical intelligence.

The Department's real concern, neither clearly articulated nor readily curable by amendment, was that the DNI would use his authority, budgetary and otherwise, to alter the balance of military and antiterrorist intelligence-gathering efforts in favor of the latter. Not that the military is indifferent to the "war" on terrorism or even that calling it a war is inapt. But it is more concerned with threats posed by hostile or potentially hostile states (currently, the principal ones are North Korea, Iran, and China) than with the threats posed by terrorist gangs, such as al Qaeda, which are not threats that the military is particularly well equipped to deal with. The Defense Department would not like its intelligence agencies that concentrate on strategic intelligence, such as the National Security Agency (the largest of all U.S. intelligence agencies), to be deflected from gathering intelligence about the military capabilities and intentions of foreign states to gathering intelligence about terrorists.

One might have expected President Bush and Secretary of Defense Rumsfeld to be acutely responsive to this concern. But the President was trapped into supporting the 9/11 Commission's proposals by the confluence of several factors. First, within days of the issuance of the commission's report, Senator Kerry, the Democratic Presidential nominee, endorsed all its recommendations emphatically and without reservations, thereby compelling Bush, as a matter of political survival in a hard-fought campaign pivoting on national-security issues, to follow suit, lest Kerry wrest the mantle of fiercer terrorist-fighter from him. And having endorsed the commission's recommendations Bush could hardly withdraw the endorsement after winning the election, whatever his inner feelings, though acting through his congressional allies he could try to water them down, and did. Second, because the Republicans unexpectedly gained seats in both the Senate and the House of Representatives in the election, giving them firm control of the entire Congress, Bush's failure to obtain enactment of the commission's recommendations, when he had endorsed them, would have been read as weakness—an inability to control his own party, a sign that he was fast becoming a lame duck.

Third was a failure by the media to subject either the commission's recommendations or the legislative follow-up to sustained, critical scrutiny. There was some good press criticism, but it was mainly limited to editorial and op-ed pieces, necessarily of limited depth.[4] Great credit must be given to the commission's public-relations sense, if not its policy sense. The commission's bipartisan composition, its unanimity, its sentimental alliance with (or perhaps one should say exploitation of) the families of the victims of the 9/11 attacks, the rhetorical adroitness and sheer heft of its report, journalists' aversion to complex and abstract issues of public policy (mirroring and reinforcing the ignorance and indifference of the public at large), the curious lack of interest in the subject by media-adept public intellectuals, the natural reticence of intelligence officers, the unpopularity of the intelligence agencies (which makes them natural scapegoats and is one of the factors contributing to the shaky morale of intelligence officers), a sense on the part of a number of members of Congress of both parties that the President had actually done little to strengthen the

4. For examples, see Editorial, "Rush to Czardom," *Wall Street Journal*, Aug. 4, 2004, p. A12; David S. Broder, "Heeding the 9/11 Panel," *Washington Post*, Aug. 8, 2004, p. B7; Editorial, "Stampede on Intelligence," *Washington Post*, Sept. 2, 2004, p. A22; William Safire, "Tomorrow's 'Rogue Elephant,'" *New York Times* (late ed.), Sept. 8, 2004, p. A23.

intelligence system in the wake of 9/11, the timing of the release of the commission's report in the midst of the Presidential election campaign, and its ensuing endorsement by both Presidential candidates, combined to paralyze most public and private criticism and confer holy-writ status on the report, including its recommendations.

The media portrayed the legislative issue almost entirely as one of turf wars and politics: the Defense Department's largely behind-the-scenes fight to hold onto its turf and the President's need to prove his control of Congress by obtaining legislation that his own Secretary of Defense probably, as well as some members of his party (especially in the House of Representatives) certainly, opposed, without relying on the votes of Democratic members. One can speculate that the liberal media supported the legislation in part because of a reflex enthusiasm for "reform" and an instinctive aversion to the CIA—dispositions that made the idea that the intelligence system was broken and had to be fixed congenial. It is odd, though, that liberals would favor a measure intended to make the intelligence system more of a monolith; one would think they'd want to preserve some internal checks and balances by keeping the system decentralized and in particular that they would want to keep domestic and foreign intelligence separate. The idea that the CIA would engage in domestic intelligence gives even conservatives the creeps; yet the Intelligence Reform Act takes a step in that direction by placing the Director of National Intelligence over both the CIA and the domestic intelligence activity of the FBI. The liberals' support of the legislation is a sign of the political decline of the civil liberties lobby, which opposed it. The conservative media supported it because they favor strengthening national security, which was the basis on which the legislation was marketed by its sponsors and supporters.

A fourth possibility is that the President swallowed any

doubts he may have had about the organizational provisions of the new act because he thought them likely to prove inconsequential in operation—the common fate of government reorganizations, as we'll see in Chapter 5. The Director of National Intelligence will be an executive branch official appointed by and serving at the pleasure of the President. Although he is not to be part of the Executive Office of the President, so that he won't be enveloped in the intensely political atmosphere of a President's staff, an official who serves at the pleasure of the President exercises as much or as little power as the President wishes. So the DNI may end up weaker than the 9/11 Commission or even Congress envisaged.

The President may have felt that, as a practical matter, the elaborate structural provisions of the Intelligence Reform Act do little more than delete the section of the National Security Act of 1947 that makes the Director of Central Intelligence also the head of the Central Intelligence Agency.[5] With just that deletion, the President—if he wanted, by delegating more power to the Director of Central Intelligence, to tighten central control of the intelligence system in order to improve coordination among the intelligence agencies—could have freed up the director's time for the exercise of new powers by appointing another person to head the CIA, thus relieving the DCI of responsibility for the agency's day-to-day operations.

One thing the President might want to do would be to make the FBI's domestic intelligence service one of the services that a DCI coordinates. Because of the taboo that I just mentioned against the CIA's operating against targets in the United States, domestic intelligence has not been under even the loose supervision that the DCI exercises over intelligence programs outside the CIA, since the Director of Central Intelligence is also

5. National Security Act of 1947, § 102(a)(3), 50 U.S.C. § 403(a)(3).

the Director of the Central Intelligence Agency. These sound almost like synonyms. If the two jobs were separated (and perhaps the Director of Central Intelligence renamed the Director of Intelligence to eliminate the echo of the CIA in the name), the taboo would fall away. An independent reason to separate them is that it would eliminate the conflict of interest inherent in having one person both control one intelligence agency and exercise authority, albeit limited, over the agencies that compete with "his" agency for appropriations.

Even without such an amendment, the President could have gone a long way toward freeing the DCI from most of his day-to-day responsibilities as CIA director simply by appointing a superlative manager as a second deputy director or by strengthening the position of the agency's executive director (chief operating officer). Also without new legislation the President could have run proposed candidates to head the various intelligence agencies by the DCI, asked him to coordinate the agencies' budget proposals, given him a sizable staff, and, in short, accomplished by executive order most of the aims of the new legislation. Precedents exist for such executive reorganizing of the intelligence system, as we know from Chapter 1.

Indeed—though this has largely been overlooked—President Bush had already taken several steps in that direction in a pair of executive orders that he issued on August 27, 2004, in response to the 9/11 Commission's report and before the bills that culminated in the Intelligence Reform Act were introduced in Congress. One of these orders made the DCI "the principal adviser to the President for intelligence matters related to the national security," tasked him with developing "objectives and guidance for the Intelligence Community necessary, in the Director's judgment, to ensure timely and effective collection, processing, analysis, and dissemination of intelligence, of whatever nature and from whatever source derived," and

directed him to "establish common security and access standards for managing and handling intelligence," "establish,
operate, and direct national centers of intelligence," "establish
policies, procedures, and mechanisms that translate intelligence objectives and priorities approved by the President into
specific guidance for the Intelligence Community," "develop,
determine, and present with the advice of the heads of departments or agencies" an annual consolidated intelligence budget,
and transfer appropriated funds among agencies.[6] The order
also gave the DCI veto power over appointments of heads of
intelligence organizations who are not Presidential appointees,
directed him to submit his own recommendation to Congress
to accompany any Presidential nomination of the head of an
intelligence service who is a Presidential appointee, and
directed him to establish standards and qualifications for intelligence personnel. Although one of the major proposals of the
9/11 Commission adopted by the Intelligence Reform Act is the
creation of a National Counterterrorism Center, the second
executive order issued by the President on August 27, 2004, had
already done that.[7]

The President would not even have needed to issue an
executive order in order to centralize authority over the intelligence agencies' budget proposals to Congress. That authority
is already centralized in the Office of Management and Budget,
which is part of the Executive Office of the President.

A striking aspect of the media's coverage of the proposed
legislation was their failure to ask why the legislation was necessary, given the President's existing authority over the orga-

6. "Strengthened Management of the Intelligence Community," Executive
Order 13355, 69 Fed. Reg. 53593 (Aug. 27, 2004).

7. "National Counterterrorism Center," Executive Order 13354, 69 Fed.
Reg. 53589 (Aug. 27, 2004).

nization and budget of the intelligence system and his exercise of that authority in the August executive orders.

The President may have issued those orders in anticipation of the Intelligence Reform Act rather than because he thought such a revamping of the existing structure a good idea. He may even have hoped to preempt the act; so maybe the act should be viewed as a prod to prevent his backtracking from the executive orders. (More likely, it is an attempt by the 9/11 Commission and its congressional supporters to take credit for fixing the intelligence system.) How effective a prod remains to be seen. If the President resists, because he doesn't want as much centralization as Congress wants, he has only to pick a Director of National Intelligence who will delegate as much authority to the individual intelligence services as they have traditionally enjoyed. The only obstacle to this devolution of the DNI's authority would be that the Senate might refuse to confirm a nominee who it thought would be too pliant a tool of the President. This is unlikely to be an insurmountable obstacle even when the Senate is in the control of a different party from the President's. Only as long as there is a political consensus in favor of greater centralization of intelligence will the Intelligence Reform Act be interpreted in the spirit of the 9/11 Commission's report, and if there is such a consensus the President is likely to centralize without legislative prodding. The act itself will have little coercive force because the relevant provisions are spongy and because the inevitable disagreements over their meaning will be resolved not by the courts but by the Justice Department's Office of Legal Counsel—headed by an assistant attorney general appointed by the President. The President failed to preempt the Intelligence Reform Act, but the act may prove to have been an unsuccessful effort to preempt the President. We may be in the presence of an unedifying power struggle between the legislative and executive branches of the government.

As finally enacted, the Reform Act largely combines the organizational provisions of the Senate bill, somewhat modified at the urging of the Bush administration, and the nonorganizational recommendations of the 9/11 Commission, with the domestic law enforcement add-ons in the House bill, though some of these, such as the ban on issuing drivers' licenses to illegal immigrants, were dropped—that particular one presumably because of opposition from Hispanics, an interest group courted by both parties.[8] The principal alterations to the organizational provisions in the Senate bill dilute the authority of the Director of National Intelligence—strikingly so in contrast to the 9/11 Commission's recommendations. The act gives with one hand and takes away with the other. The DNI is to "serve as head of the intelligence community"—but he is to do so "subject to the authority, direction, and control of the President."[9] (Moreover, his predecessor, the Director of Central Intelligence, was also designated to "serve as head of the intelligence community,"[10] yet that designation was thought inadequate by the 9/11 Commission and Congress to define the position they envisaged.) The DNI is to "oversee and direct the implementation of the National Intelligence Program [i.e., the overall federal intelligence budget minus the budget for tactical military intelligence]."[11] But he is to do so "consistent with"

8. For a helpful summary of the act, see U.S. Senate Committee on Governmental Affairs, "Summary of Intelligence Reform and Terrorism Prevention Act of 2004" (Dec. 6, 2004).

9. National Security Act of 1947, § 102(b)(1), 50 U.S.C. § 403(a)(1), added by Intelligence Reform and Terrorism Prevention Act of 2004, Title I, § 1011(a).

10. National Security Act of 1947, § 102(a), 50 U.S.C. § 403(a).

11. On what exactly is excluded under the heading of tactical military intelligence, see discussion in Chapter 5. The predecessor to the National Intelli-

Presidential guidelines designed to ensure that he "respects and does not abrogate the statutory responsibilities of the heads of the departments of the United States Government concerning such departments,"[12] including of course the Defense Department, which owns the major intelligence agencies.

The DNI is to provide "guidance" in the formulation of budget requests by the agencies whose budgets are part of the National Intelligence Program, and having received their requests he is to formulate a consolidated budget for submission "to the President for approval"[13]—which means that the President will submit the budget to Congress with whatever changes in it *he* wants to make. Once it goes to Congress it will be split up among the various congressional appropriations committees, just as before the act, since the act does not alter the existing system of congressional oversight. (That in any event is an internal matter for each house of Congress to determine, rather than a subject for legislation; at this writing, it is unclear whether either house will alter its system of intelligence oversight significantly.) The DNI is, however, given authority to make limited reallocations of appropriated funds among agencies. As I said in the first chapter, it is unclear whether streamlining the legislative oversight process would weaken or strengthen the DNI's hand, but probably it would strengthen it.

The Reform Act limits the DNI's authority over personnel. Appointments of heads of the departmental intelligence ser-

gence Program was the National Foreign Intelligence Program. "Foreign" has been dropped because the NIP, unlike the NFIP, includes the budget for domestic intelligence.

12. Intelligence Reform and Terrorism Prevention Act of 2004, Title I, § 1011(a), adding National Security Act of 1947, § 102(b)(3), 50 U.S.C. § 403(b)(3); § 1018.

13. Id., § 1011(a), adding National Security Act of 1947, §102A(c)(1)(C) 50 U.S.C. § 403A(c)(1)(C).

vices who are not Presidential appointees, such as the head of
the FBI's intelligence division, require his concurrence, but
he does not nominate candidates for these positions. In the
case of heads of intelligence services who are Presidential appointees, the DNI's concurrence in a recommendation to the
President by the departmental head (for example, a recommendation by the Secretary of State for a nominee as Assistant
Secretary of State for Intelligence and Research) is also
required, but this seems pretty empty. There is also a constitutional question as to whether Congress can circumscribe the
President's appointive powers in the ways the act attempts to
do, but I will not pursue it.[14]

I noted in the first chapter the 9/11 Commission's fascina-
tion with the Goldwater-Nichols Act as a model for reforming
the intelligence system. I compared the DNI to the Secretary of
Defense but also noted the DNI's lack of comparable command
authority. This raises questions that the Intelligence Reform
Act does not answer, such as: If the CIA director is planning an
operation that the DNI considers dumb, what can the latter do?
Can he order the CIA director to cancel the operation? Or must
he go to the President and advise the President to order it can-
celed? If he must go the latter route, as seems to be the case
(for though the Intelligence Reform Act requires the director
of the CIA to report to the DNI rather than to the President, the
authority to issue operational orders to the CIA remains with
the President), can he really be considered the "head of the
intelligence community"? The Chairman of the Joint Chiefs of

14. See, for example, "Common Legislative Encroachments on Executive
Branch Authority," Lexsee 1989 OLC Lexis 1988 (Opinion of the Office of Legal
Counsel, U.S. Department of Justice, July 27, 1989). It is true that the Presidential executive order that I cited in note 6 limits the President's appointive
authority even more, but that is a voluntary limitation (more precisely a delegation of authority), which the President can revoke at any time.

Staff is the President's principal military adviser, but he is not the head of the armed forces; the President, and in most matters the Secretary of Defense, is. Who, then, is the head of the intelligence system? And if the DNI is not really the head, what exactly is he? What happened to the adage that too many cooks spoil the broth? Or to Napoleon's dictum that the only thing worse than one bad general is two good ones?

Another unresolved issue, mundane but important, is the DNI's responsibility for liaison with foreign intelligence services. No other democratic nation, as far as I know, has such an official—democratic nations, including the United States before the Intelligence Reform Act, have shied away from placing the same official in charge of both foreign and domestic intelligence, lest the rough methods used by intelligence services on foreigners in foreign, often hostile, countries be turned on citizens. Will the heads of the CIA, the NSA, the FBI's domestic intelligence service, and the others continue to "liaise" with their counterparts in the other countries, or is the DNI to step into that role? The question is important because the word "liaison" does not adequately convey the degree to which our intelligence services, especially the CIA, depend on assistance from foreign intelligence services, because so many terrorists bent on harming the United States reside abroad. The CIA obtains the assistance of the "liaison" services, as they are called, in many of the smaller countries by providing technical and other assistance

The DNI is authorized to have a staff of 500. Almost all of them will come from the existing agencies, certainly in the near term. This transfer of personnel is likely to produce serious disarray in the intelligence community, though this may depend on the composition of the staff. Doubtless it will include many auditors, lawyers, publicists, reviewers, and other bureaucratic barnacles. But probably it will be composed mainly of intelligence analysts. That may be worse. The Reform Act leaves the relation between the analyst staff of the CIA and the analyst staff (if any) of the DNI undefined. But the former may atrophy if the latter, being higher in the bureaucratic pecking order, establishes itself as the dominant source of intelligence analysis. That would be like placing the CIA's collectors of intelligence and its analysts in separate agencies, Senator Roberts's questionable proposal. What is to be collected depends to an important degree on what the analysts identify as relevant and important. The closest coordination is necessary. It is ironic that a statute intended to improve coordination should risk imperiling it.

The organizational provisions are the subject of Titles I and II of the Reform Act, out of eight titles in all. The two titles contain an impressive 27,000 words (out of the act's total of 99,000). Yet most of the provisions, besides the few I have mentioned, are either bureaucratic flyspecking, such as the provision that any reference to the Director of Central Intelligence "in any law, regulation, document, paper, or other record of the United States shall be deemed to be a reference to the Director of the Central Intelligence Agency,"[15] because the DCI has now been replaced by the DNI, or fatuous exhortations, such as that "the Director of National Intelligence shall ensure the elimination of waste and unnecessary duplication within the intelligence community."[16] The inclusion of such empty rhetoric makes it difficult to take the legislative process that produced the Intelligence Reform Act seriously.

15. Intelligence Reform and Terrorism Prevention Act of 2004, Title I, § 1081(b). The only real change of nomenclature that the act needed to make— but didn't—was to rename the CIA the Foreign Intelligence Service, since it is no longer the "central" intelligence agency. The center is now occupied by the Director of National Intelligence and his staff.

16. Id., § 1011(a), adding National Security Act of 1947, § 102A(f)(5), 50 U.S.C. § 403A(f)(5).

As far as the new structure of the intelligence system is concerned, only two things emerge with clarity from this immensely complex piece of legislation rushed through Congress with such unseemly haste.[17] One is that the legislation somewhat blunts the centralizing thrust of the 9/11 Commission's report. The key word is "somewhat." The extent of centralization accomplished by the act will emerge in the process of implementation and will depend primarily on decisions made by the President. The analysis in Part II of this book is intended to contribute to what will undoubtedly be a protracted struggle over implementation. The system created by the legislation is, let us hope, plastic;[18] for the alternative is that it is molasses.

Second, although the legislation does not adopt the 9/11 Commission's recommendation to strip the CIA of its paramilitary capability, it does envision the weakening of the agency. There will be a DNI with potentially large powers and a large staff perhaps drawn largely from the CIA. The National Counterterrorism Center will report to the DNI rather than to the CIA's director and is likely to be staffed heavily with officers from the CIA, particularly from the CIA's Counterterrorism Center, which indeed the NCTC may largely supersede. The National Intelligence Council, a small but prestigious intelligence unit that issues the influential National Intelligence Esti-

17. As argued persuasively by Senator Byrd. Robert C. Byrd, "Politics Surround Intelligence Reform," *YubaNet.com*, Dec. 9, 2004, at www.yubanet.com/artman/publish/printer 16024.shtml.

18. "The Congress has almost certainly created years of turbulence at every level of the intelligence community but its legislation has not done that much harm. The right leaders with the right priorities can make the new system work, just as they could have made the old system work . . . Everything will depend on what Congress in its reforms largely ignored or dealt with in terms of meaningless exhortations." Anthony Cordesman, "The US Needs Intelligence Reform," *FT.com*, Jan. 6, 2006, p. 1, at proquest.umi.com/pqdlink?did=775131741&sid=1&Fmt=3&clientld=13392&RQT=309&Vname=PQD.

mates, will now report to the DNI rather than to the Director of Central Intelligence. NIC was not in the CIA, but it is likely to become more competitive with the CIA when it no longer reports to a person who doubles as DCI and DCIA. Competition between intelligence agencies is a good thing, as I shall argue in Chapter 5; here I want merely to note the extent to which the CIA is to take the hit for the failure to prevent the 9/11 attacks.

All the other components of national defense against terrorism that failed on 9/11 are to be strengthened, although many of them, notably the FBI, failed worse than the CIA did. This curious result may have a political explanation. The CIA, especially in contrast to the FBI, is an unpopular agency. One reason is that spying and other clandestine operations are regarded in some quarters as dirty business. But a more important reason is the psychological asymmetry of failure and success in intelligence operations. If the CIA fails to anticipate a surprise attack or some other surprising event, the failure is palpable; the attack, or the event, occurs and is observed, and its consequences felt. But if the CIA succeeds in anticipating the attack or the event, which as a result is averted, then the success, even if it is publicly disclosed (usually it will not be), will fail to make a dramatic impact because nothing observable has happened.[19] The success was, precisely, that nothing happened—and it's hard to get excited about nothing; it requires an exercise of imagination to visualize a disaster that is averted. So the failures of the CIA register strongly in the public mind and are remembered, and the successes forgotten, and the result is to give the agency a negative image and make it an attractive scapegoat.

19. This distinction is an aspect of what cognitive psychologists call the "availability heuristic," which I discuss in Chapter 4.

I mentioned the media's failure to subject the 9/11 Commission's recommendations and Congress's deliberations to critical scrutiny. Exhibiting its propensity to look on the dark side of the news, as soon as the House and Senate resolved their differences and passage of the Intelligence Reform Act became assured, the press woke up and discovered that the act wasn't a panacea after all. The day after Congress approved it the *New York Times* began to wonder whether "the changes will make much of a difference. . . . On that question, even some supporters of the legislation to overhaul intelligence acknowledge their own agnosticism. . . . The changes that will matter most still lie ahead."[20] The article quotes one former official as having "found considerable 'confusion and contradiction' within the intelligence bill." Although the DNI is described as "the one figure unquestionably in charge of a sprawling enterprise that is now often only loosely coordinated," "in other ways" he "will be constrained in the ability to wield that authority, operating at an altitude a further bureaucratic step removed from spies, analysts and others on whom intelligence successes and failures ultimately depend." After reporting a comment by a former official that "by putting someone above the fray, you leave him without a day-to-day window into what any of the agencies are really doing," the article remarks surprisingly that "the most significant benefit of the new structure" may be to improve the management of the nation's spy satellite programs. Yet it is difficult to see how the DNI will be able to focus on that matter, where friction with the Defense Department will be at its maximum, when he is supposed to be the President's principal intelligence adviser plus the coordinator in chief of the entire intelligence system.

20. Douglas Jehl, "The Spymaster Question," *New York Times* (late ed.), Dec. 8, 2004, p. A28.

Part II

Toward the Optimal Organization of the U.S. Intelligence System

Chapter 3

The History and Anatomy of Successful Surprise Attacks

We have seen how the 9/11 Commission approached the question of the optimal organization of the U.S. intelligence system, and how Congress followed the approach, though at a distance, producing considerable uncertainty as to how the system will actually change. In this and the following chapters I consider from the ground up the soundness of alternative organizational approaches. Part of the grounding for such an analysis is the history of surprise attacks, because it is the fear of such attacks (another 9/11) that has powered the drive for reorganization. Surprise attacks, I argue in this chapter, follow a pattern, and the 9/11 attacks conformed to it. Once the pattern is understood, the question of whether reorganizing our intelligence system is a sensible response to the threat of such attacks will be focused more sharply than the commission or Congress succeeded in focusing it.

Before 9/11, the biggest surprise attack on the United States had been the Japanese attack on Pearl Harbor in December 1941. That attack is the subject of a large scholarly literature rightly dominated by Roberta Wohlstetter's classic study.[1] Although it was published more than 40 years ago and additional documents relating to why we were surprised have been declassified or have otherwise become available since, and although a stubborn revisionist literature argues that Roosevelt or Churchill or both knew the attack was coming but kept mum in order to get America into the war, Wohlstetter's study is generally and, so far as I can judge, correctly considered authoritative.[2]

As she explains, we had plenty of warning signs of an impending attack, in part because we had cracked the code ("MAGIC") that the Japanese government used to communicate with its embassies around the world, including its embassy in Washington. War with Japan was expected to break out at any time, and Pearl Harbor was known to be within range of the Japanese fleet, which was rich in aircraft carriers. The direction of a Japanese offensive on the outbreak of war was

1. Roberta Wohlstetter, *Pearl Harbor: Warning and Decision* (1962). The subsequent scholarship on surprise attacks includes Cynthia M. Grabo, *Anticipating Surprise: Analysis for Strategic Warning* (2002); Ephraim Kam, *Surprise Attack: The Victim's Perspective* (1988); Ariel Levite, *Intelligence and Strategic Surprises* (1987); Richard K. Betts, *Surprise Attack: Lessons for Defense Planning* (1982); James J. Wirtz, "Theory of Surprise," in *Paradoxes of Strategic Intelligence: Essays in Honor of Michael I. Handel* 101 (Richard K. Betts and Thomas G. Mahnken, eds., 2003); Wesley Wark, "Intelligence Predictions and Strategic Surprise: Reflections on the British Experience in the 1930s," in *British and American Approaches to Intelligence* 85 (K. G. Robertson, ed., 1987); Gerald W. Hopple, "Intelligence and Warning: Implications and Lessons of the Falkland Islands War," 36 *World Politics* 339 (1984); Steve Chan, "The Intelligence of Stupidity: Understanding Failures in Strategic Warning," 73 *American Political Science Review* 171 (1979). See also "Appendix: Empirical Studies of Strategic Surprise: A Bibliography," in Levite, above, at 189–190.

2. See, for example, Richard K. Betts, "Surprise, Scholasticism, and Strategy: A Review of Ariel Levite's *Intelligence and Strategic Surprises* (1987)," 33 *International Studies Quarterly* 329, 334–335 (1989); John Costello, *The Pacific War* 608 (1981); Colby Cosh, "Whose Infamy?" *Report/Newsmagazine*, June 25, 2001, p. 46.

expected to be southward, toward the Philippines, Malaya, and the Dutch East Indies (now Indonesia), and such an offensive would expose the Japanese flank to an attack by the U.S. Pacific fleet, which was stationed at Pearl Harbor; an attack on Pearl Harbor would therefore remove a threat to the offensive.[3]

Why, then, were measures not taken to protect Pearl Harbor from a carrier-based air attack? The answer, as Wohlstetter explains, is multifold:

To have a reasonable chance of detecting a surprise attack would have required dense air patrols that would have stripped aircraft from other fronts that seemed in greater danger of attack, such as the Philippines—which in fact was attacked within hours of Pearl Harbor—and would have interfered with pilot training. When a satisfactory response to a threat is difficult to devise, the tendency is, ostrich-like, to deny the threat. Similarly, because our fleet was already heavily engaged in combat with German submarines in the Atlantic (though we were not yet formally at war with Germany), it was difficult to see how we could take on Japan at the same time; "the assumption was . . . 'If we lose in the Atlantic, we lose everywhere.' This meant that the Far East simply had to stay quiet."[4]

Although some signs pointed to a possible attack on Pearl Harbor, more pointed to other possible Japanese military objectives, including the Soviet Union—where an attack by the Japanese from the east would have been a logical complement to the German invasion of the Soviet Union from the west—and Thailand, and the British, Dutch, and U.S. possessions in the Far East. (However, by the end of October 1941, the Siberian climate had probably foreclosed a Japanese attack on the Soviet Union.) "We failed to anticipate Pearl Harbor not for want of

3. Wohlstetter, note 1 above, at 368, 373, 387.
4. Id. at 273.

the relevant materials, but because of a plethora of irrelevant ones. Much of the appearance of wanton neglect that emerged in various investigations of the disaster resulted from the unconscious suppression of vast congeries of signs pointing in every direction except Pearl Harbor."[5] "The signals that the local commanders later argued were muffled and fraught with uncertainty are the ones they viewed before the event. The signals that seem to stand out and scream of the impending catastrophe are the ones learned about only after the event, when they appear stripped of other possible meanings."[6]

In part because the warning signals were so numerous and in part because they were not effectively pooled, no one had the full picture of the danger. One reason the signals weren't pooled was security. The best source, the decrypted MAGIC code, was highly sensitive because if the Japanese discovered that their code had been broken they would change it. So access to MAGIC was limited to a handful of high officials— who had neither the time nor the background to make sense of what they were reading.[7]

Our leaders had difficulty understanding *why* the Japanese would want to attack Pearl Harbor. It is true that we were squeezing Japan hard economically, in part to deter it from attacking the Soviet Union but also to compel it to abandon its ambition to dominate Asia.[8] But we were unlikely to attack Japan unless it attacked us. Japan was so much weaker than the United States that its optimal strategy, one would have thought, was to try to avoid precipitating a war. Had Japan confined its aggression to nations it could actually defeat, the

5. Id. at 387.
6. Id. at 226.
7. Id. at 394.
8. John J. Mearsheimer, *The Tragedy of Great Power Politics* 222–223 (2001).

United States might—given its strong isolationist streak and the Roosevelt administration's preoccupation with the greater menace of Nazi Germany—have hesitated to declare war on Japan. To understand why the Japanese might nevertheless decide to attack Pearl Harbor would have required us to understand a culture alien to our own—concretely, to understand that although the Japanese knew they'd probably be defeated in a war with the United States, they thought it more honorable to fight a losing war than abandon their announced policy of dominating Asia. We would also have had to understand how Japan's rulers thought the United States would react to such an attack. We underestimated their devotion to national honor, and they underestimated ours.[9]

An intelligence consensus is difficult to challenge with new data because people are reluctant to change their minds—to admit to having been mistaken and to being surprised, which could hurt their careers by giving them a reputation for being unsteady and unreliable.[10] There are career risks in challenging even a consensus one hasn't helped to form: "one index to sound judgment is agreement with the hypotheses on which current department policy is based."[11] The consensus was that the danger to Pearl Harbor in the event of war with Japan was sabotage by Japanese agents recruited from the part of the Hawaiian population that was of Japanese ethnicity. To warn of an air attack would have been to challenge that consensus.

On several occasions before the attack, there were credible warnings that war with Japan was about to break out, and

9. Wohlstetter, note 1 above, at 355.
10. Canice Prendergast and Lars Stole, "Impetuous Youngsters and Jaded Old-Timers: Acquiring a Reputation for Learning," 104 *Journal of Political Economy* 1105 (1996).
11. Wohlstetter, note 1 above, at 302. Cf. Canice Prendergast, "A Theory of 'Yes Men,'" 83 *American Economic Review* 757 (1993).

when it did not intelligence officers were reluctant to repeat such warnings lest they be thought alarmists. Also, a peak of alertness is bound to be followed by a trough.[12] People cannot keep themselves at peak alert all the time; they get tired. The more false alarms there are, the shorter and lower the peaks and the deeper and longer the troughs. Warnings issued by Washington, moreover, may not be taken seriously by local commanders, especially if previous alerts have proved to be a waste of time and resources because they were induced by false alarms. The locals may feel they have better insight into the situation than remote officials. The army and navy commanders in Hawaii were warned on the eve of the Pearl Harbor attack that war was about to break out with Japan, but their response, in line with the consensus noted above, was to redouble their efforts to prevent sabotage. Unhappily some of the measures taken, such as parking airplanes closer together to make them easier to guard, increased our vulnerability to an attack from the air. Also, the last-minute warnings were vague: the local commanders were ordered to place their forces on alert, but there are different degrees of alert and Washington failed to specify which degree the commanders should order.[13]

Finally, there was no overall commander of U.S. forces in Hawaii. The army and navy commanders reported only to their superiors in their own service. There was no joint army-navy staff either, and the office of Chairman of the Joint Chiefs of Staff did not yet exist. There were War and Navy Departments, but the War Department was simply the army department; there was no Department of Defense. The army and navy had separate intelligence services, and the sharing of information between them was poor.[14] There was no counterpart to the CIA

12. Wohlstetter, note 1 above, at 398.
13. Id. at 138–139.
14. Id. at 98, 163, 273.

(not created until 1947) or the Defense Intelligence Agency (1961), and thus no "center for evaluating a mass of conflicting signals from specialized or partisan sources."[15] Missing too was any procedure for synthesizing confidential with public sources of information about enemy intentions and capabilities.[16] This was regrettable because "in comparing the top-secret Intelligence evaluations of enemy intentions with estimates in the contemporary press, one is struck by the relative soundness of the less privileged judgments. It is hard not to conclude that general knowledgeability in the world of international affairs, and close observation of overt developments, are the most useful ingredients in making such estimates."[17]

The organizational problems were eventually corrected by the creation of the Defense Department, the CIA, and the DIA. No one has devised satisfactory correctives for the other problems that Wohlstetter identified, as a few more examples will illustrate.

At the end of January 1968, during the Tet holiday period, the United States was stunned by an offensive mounted by Viet Cong and North Vietnamese forces against South Vietnam's cities. As with the Pearl Harbor attack, signs of the impending offensive abounded. Indeed, through a communications mix-up some Viet Cong jumped the gun and attacked several South Vietnamese cities the day before the holiday period began.[18] That should have been recognized as conclusive corroboration of predictions of a cities offensive during Tet. Some preparatory defensive measures were taken, but it is apparent from their very limited character, and from the business-as-usual behav-

15. Id. at 130.
16. Id. at 131.
17. Id. at 169; see also id. at 131.
18. Spencer C. Tucker, *Vietnam* 138 (1999).

ior of the U.S. and South Vietnamese military commanders on the eve of Tet, that the scope and intensity of the attack came as a complete surprise.

Why?[19] As in the case of Pearl Harbor, our commanders were distracted by what seemed a greater menace—the siege of our base at Khe Sanh, in the northern part of South Vietnam,[20] where it seemed that General Giap was trying to repeat his victory over the French at Dien Bien Phu in the first Vietnam war. This preconception led the U.S. command to interpret signs of preparation for an attack on South Vietnam's cities as preparations for a mere diversionary attack designed to trick the United States into shifting troops away from Khe Sanh. We might have had a similar reaction had the Japanese planted clues that they were planning to attack Pearl Harbor.

It seemed unlikely that the enemy would try, as it did, to take over South Vietnam's cities. That would exceed the aim of a diversionary attack. Anyway the enemy seemed too weak to achieve the more ambitious goal, just as the Japanese were too weak to take on the United States in a war. The enemy *was* too weak; it suffered horrendous losses in the Tet offensive and was driven out of all the cities it attacked. The offensive had a decisive effect on U.S. public opinion, but apparently this was not anticipated. Rather, the enemy thought itself strong enough, or the South Vietnamese so weak, that the offensive would end the war by causing the South Vietnamese regime to collapse. The enemy was wrong. The lesson, just as in the case of Pearl Harbor, is that "to avoid surprise, it is often necessary to anticipate the opponent's mistakes. Nations sometimes sur-

19. The discussion that follows draws mainly on James J. Wirtz, *The Tet Offensive: Intelligence Failure in War* (1991).
20. Id., ch. 5.

prise their opponents by reaching for overly ambitious objectives."[21]

Although there were skeptics, the official view of U.S. defense officials on the eve of Tet was that we were winning the war. In that light the preferred interpretation of the signs of impending attack was that, if it came and proved to be more than a mere diversionary attack, it would be a last fling, like Hitler's 1944 Ardennes attack on U.S. forces (the Battle of the Bulge), an analogy invoked explicitly by our military command. Because we had won that battle so decisively that the German attack turned out to have shortened the war by depleting the German forces, we could look forward to a Tet cities attack with equanimity. Oddly, while optimists about our prospects in the war would have been inclined to predict an unsuccessful attack, pessimists would have been inclined to predict no attack, on the ground that having stalemated us the enemy had only to wait until the American public got tired of the war and forced the United States to withdraw, as would have happened even without a Tet offensive.

We were handicapped not only by a false analogy but also by cultural ignorance. We thought the Communists wouldn't dare outrage South Vietnamese public opinion by violating the traditional Tet truce. A longer tradition, had we known it, would have cast doubt on that expectation. In 1789, when Vietnam was ruled by the hated Chinese, the Vietnamese rose in a surprise attack on their masters during Tet and won Vietnam's independence.[22] So there was a precedent for the 1968 Tet offensive. A more mundane reason for the enemy to schedule a major offensive during the Tet holiday was that almost a third of the South Vietnamese army was expected to be on holiday leave.

21. Id. at 12. See also Grabo, note 1 above, at 86.
22. Tucker, note 18 above, at 19, 136.

In short, in Vietnam we used what we knew to create a theory of what might happen during Tet. The theory was plausible, but erroneous.

My third example of a successful surprise attack before 9/11 is the attack by Egypt and Syria on Israel in 1973, on the Jewish holiday of Yom Kippur. Because the bulk of the Israeli army consists of reserve formations that require a minimum of 48 hours to mobilize and reach the front, Israel is highly vulnerable to a surprise attack. Having launched a Pearl Harbor–style surprise air attack to open the Six-Day War in 1967, Israel knew that the Arab states would be happy to return the compliment. There was no doubt who the enemies were, and their attack options were limited because of the small size of Israel (even with the occupied territories): if they attacked, it would be across the Suez Canal into Sinai and across the cease-fire line in the Golan Heights. As is typical of surprise attacks, warnings that an attack was coming were abundant but were waved aside, and Egypt and Syria achieved surprise.

The reasons for their success in surprising Israel were investigated at length by the Agranat Commission, an ad hoc committee of notables, not unlike the 9/11 Commission.[23] From its report we learn that the military intelligence branch of the Israeli armed forces, the only intelligence agency responsible for assessing threats of invasion, was convinced that Egypt and

23. For the relevant portions of the Agranat Commission's report, see "Israel: What Went Wrong on October 6? The Partial Report of the Israeli Commission of Inquiry into the October War," 3 *Journal of Palestine Studies* 189 (1974). See also Uri Bar-Joseph, "Intelligence Failure and the Need for Cognitive Closure: The Case of Yom Kippur," in *Paradoxes of Strategic Intelligence*, note 1 above, at 166; Michael I. Handel, *Perception, Deception and Surprise: The Case of the Yom Kippur War* (1976); Avi Shlaim, "Failures in National Intelligence Estimates: The Case of the Yom Kippur War," 28 *World Politics* 348 (1976).

Syria knew they were too weak to prevail in a war with Israel, just as the United States at the time of Pearl Harbor had been convinced that Japan knew it was too weak to prevail in a war with the United States. In both cases the potential victim thought that its enemy needed more time to gain the strength necessary to be able to mount a successful attack. In addition, there had been a number of false alarms. Only a few months earlier Israel had mobilized at great expense in response to a warning that it was about to be attacked. The chief of military intelligence predicted that there would be no attack, and because he was correct in that instance his prediction that there would be no Yom Kippur attack persuaded the Israeli Cabinet despite the warning signs. An excessively self-confident man, this general imposed his views on his underlings; he did not encourage debate or disagreement.

The fact that mobilization was both expensive and potentially provocative (the Arab states might think Israel was about to attack them) created a predisposition to disregard the warning signs. Concern with the provocative character of defensive measures had also figured in Stalin's notorious failure to take preventive measures against Hitler's attack on the Soviet Union in June 1941, despite hundreds of warnings. He feared that taking such measures might provoke (more likely accelerate) an attack, either by making Germany think that it was about to be attacked or, more likely, by threatening to alter the balance of power in favor of the Soviet Union, which would be less vulnerable to a successful attack once it completed its defensive measures.[24]

Although Israel's one-sided victory in the 1967 war had bred excessive contempt for its enemies—illustrating the Duke of Wellington's adage that a great victory is a great danger—

24. Betts, note 1 above, at 36–39; Betts, note 2 above, at 341–342.

Israeli intelligence was correct in thinking that Egypt and Syria were still too weak to beat Israel. Just as with America's evaluation of Japanese thinking in 1941, however, Israel misunderstood its enemies' goals: Egypt and Syria could "win" just by fighting Israel to a draw.

Reposing excessive confidence in the accuracy of its intelligence, Israel had no plan for fighting off a full-scale attack that took place before its reserves could be mobilized. And just as in the earlier surprise attacks that I have discussed, when realization finally dawned on the Israeli leaders that the nation was about to be attacked, the few hours that remained were squandered, so that full mobilization was delayed and the frontline units were not adequately alerted to the impending attack.

The Agranat Commission placed much of the blame for the fiasco on the incompetence of particular individuals, including the chief of military intelligence, his principal assistant, and the chief of the general staff. But it also criticized the structure of Israeli intelligence as excessively centralized.[25] The chief of military intelligence was also the Cabinet's principal intelligence adviser; his was the only opinion on the likelihood of surprise attacks that the Cabinet heard. The commission made a number of recommendations "designed to assure pluralism in the various types of intelligence evaluation,"[26] the principal one being to appoint a civilian intelligence adviser to the prime minister. The recommendation was ironic in view of the conclusion of the 9/11 Commission that the U.S. intelligence community is too decentralized. The Agranat Commission was

25. "Partial Report," note 23 above, at 194, 197, 199. See also Shlaim, note 23 above, at 368. These are related points. Decentralization reduces the impact of any given individual's ability on outcomes. Raaj Sah, "Fallibility in Human Organizations and Political Systems," *Journal of Economic Perspectives*, spring 1991, pp. 67, 69–71.

26. "Partial Report," note 23 above, at 199–200.

proposing the kind of intelligence structure that Congress and the 9/11 Commission thought had let us down![27] And not for the first time; our "pluralist" intelligence system failed, just like Israel's centralized one, to foresee the Yom Kippur attack.[28]

A sample of four (Pearl Harbor, Tet, Yom Kippur, 9/11) is too small to provide convincing evidence that successful surprise attacks have common features, but it is suggestive and could easily be augmented from the literature on surprise attacks.[29] The common features of the attacks I've discussed are worth stressing: the attacker was too weak to have much hope of prevailing, at least in conventional military terms; the victim's perception of the enemy's weakness contributed to failing to anticipate the attack; more broadly, the victim lacked a deep understanding of the attacker's intentions and capabilities, and so based his expectations of what the attacker would do on what he, the victim, would have done in the attacker's place;[30] the victim reasonably thought the principal danger lay elsewhere or in the future (both, in the case of the Pearl Harbor attack); the victim interpreted warning signs to fit a preconceived conception of the enemy's intentions and capabilities; the victim was lulled by false alarms or deliberate deception (as in Tet); the victim was in a state of denial concerning those forms of attack that would be hardest to defend against; intelligence officers were reluctant for career reasons to challenge their superiors' opinion; and warnings to local commanders of

27. Richard K. Betts, "Analysis, War, and Decision: Why Intelligence Failures are Inevitable," 31 *World Politics* 61, 73 and n. 30 (1978).

28. Betts, note 1 above, at 288.

29. See note 1 above.

30. Gregory F. Treverton, *Reshaping National Intelligence for an Age of Information* 4–5 (2001); Klaus Knorr, "Failures in National Intelligence Estimates: The Case of the Cuban Missiles," 16 *World Politics* 455, 464 (1964). Knorr also mentions the difficulty of basing predictions on the assumption that your enemy will blunder, although blunders are frequent.

an impending attack lacked clarity and credibility. Senator Collins, the sponsor, as we know, of the bill that eventually emerged as the Intelligence Reform Act, has been quoted as saying that "just as the National Security Act of 1947 [which established the CIA] was passed to prevent another Pearl Harbor, the Intelligence Reform Act will help us prevent another 9/11."[31] She overlooked the fact that 9/11 *was* another Pearl Harbor.

Although deficiencies in the organization of U.S. intelligence may have contributed to the success of the Pearl Harbor attack (in particular the lack of a unified command in Hawaii and the lack of a joint military intelligence agency, like the later-created Defense Intelligence Agency) and of the Yom Kippur attack (Israel relied excessively on the opinion of one intelligence officer), it is uncertain whether in either case the contribution was decisive. Among the common features of successful surprise attacks that I have listed, the structure of the victim's intelligence system is not salient.

Moreover, the causes of vulnerability to surprise attack seem intractable. This is especially true for a country like the United States that faces a multitude of potential enemies, including enemies such as al Qaeda that have a much larger range of potential targets than Japan did in 1941. It is impossible to be strong everywhere, or to respond to every alarm with costly defensive measures (such as grounding all civil aviation, as in the wake of 9/11), or to eavesdrop on every plotter. Thus, the fact that using hijacked planes as missiles was known well in advance of 9/11 to be a possible terrorist tactic[32] did not lead to taking defensive measures because the possibility

31. David S. Cloud, "Senate Passes Intelligence Bill, Sending It to White House," *Wall Street Journal*, Dec. 9, 2004, p. A4.

32. Steven Komarow and Tom Squitieri, "NORAD Had Drills Eerily Like Sept. 11," *USA Today*, Apr. 19, 2004, p. 1A; Tom Clancy, *Debt of Honor* (1997).

was remote and effective measures would have been very costly.

The inherent difficulties of defending against surprise attack are the theme of the rest of this chapter. I will use some simple math in my argument; the mathless reader can read around it.

In the language of cost-benefit analysis, the benefits of avoiding a disaster must, before they can be compared to the costs of prevention, be discounted (multiplied) by the probability that the disaster will actually occur if no additional measures are taken to prevent it. The lower the perceived probability of attack, and the less harm the attack will do if it occurs, and the higher the costs of preventive measures, including the costs created by false alarms, the less likely the measures are to be taken. To illustrate, if an attack that has a probability of .01 would, if it occurs, cause $1 billion in damage (not necessarily monetary damage), so that in the terminology of cost-benefit analysis the "expected cost" was $10 million, and the probability of the attack could be reduced to zero by taking a precaution that would cost $5 million, the precaution should be taken, because $5 million is less than $10 million (.01 × $1 billion). Alter the estimates for probability of attack, damage from attack, or cost (or efficacy) of precautionary measures, and the conclusion will be strengthened or weakened.

Consider two states of the world. In one, a warning of a surprise attack occurs but is disregarded, so the attack takes place, inflicting costs of a on the victim. In the other, the warning is heeded and the attack is defeated, at cost d (for defensive measure), but because the attack is defeated a is zero. Let the probability of the attack be p; then the probability that there will be no attack is $1 - p$. The expected cost of the attack if the warning is disregarded is therefore pa and the expected cost if the warning is heeded is $(1-p)d$, so the warning should be heeded if $pa > (1-p)d$ and disregarded otherwise.

The assumption that d affects a but not p may seem questionable because we usually think of defensive measures as being designed to reduce the likelihood of whatever prospective injury is being defended against. Most surprise attacks, however, occur even if the element of surprise is lost; they just do less damage. But the analysis would not be materially altered by assuming that defensive measures reduce the probability of an attack as well as the damage from it.

Another assumption is that if the warning is heeded, the damage inflicted by the surprise attack will be zero. This assumption is unrealistic and should be relaxed. The damage will just be smaller than if the warning had been ignored. Denote that diminished damage by b; it is smaller the greater is d, the expenditure on defensive measures when the warning is heeded.

Besides the direct cost of defensive measures, there is a lulling ("boy crying wolf") cost, which I'll denote by w. This cost is greater the smaller the probability of attack and therefore the more often that warnings will be false alarms, which increase the likelihood that true alarms will be ignored. It is also greater the greater d is, because if heavy costs are incurred to defend against an attack that does not occur there will be a greater reluctance to heed the next warning.

In light of these adjustments, the earlier inequality ($pa > (1-p)d$), which states the condition for when a warning should be heeded and thus defensive measures taken, becomes, with a slight rearrangement of terms,

$$\frac{p}{1-p} > \frac{b(d) + d + w(p,d)}{a}. \tag{1}$$

Inequality (1) says that it is more likely that heeding the warning will be the prudent response the higher p is (which not only increases the left-hand side of the inequality, but, because of its negative effect on w, reduces the right-hand side), the lower d is, the lower w is, and the higher a is. Conversely, the lower p is but the higher d is, and the smaller the effect of defensive measures in reducing b (the diminished cost of an attack if the defensive measures are taken) and hence the higher $b(d)$ is, the likelier is the prudent course to be to ignore the warning sign. The effect of d is complex: it makes heeding the warning more likely to be prudent by reducing b (the damage from the attack when precautions are taken), but less likely to be prudent because it is a cost of heeding the warning and because it increases the lulling effect.

To illustrate, the Israelis disregarded the signs of an imminent attack by the Egyptians and Syrians in October 1973 because they thought the probability of an attack low, because defensive measures (mobilization) would have been costly, because a lulling effect had been induced by a previous costly mobilization in response to what proved to be a false alarm, and because, believing that even without mobilizing the reserves their frontline forces could hold the line, they didn't think mobilization necessary to minimize the cost of an attack (i.e., they didn't think b was much lower than a). In the case of the 9/11 attacks, p was thought low, a was thought lower than it turned out to be, and d was high because of the cost, and inconvenience to passengers, of the kind of airline security measures that were adopted after the attacks.

I want to pause briefly on passenger inconvenience. One of the things that makes it especially difficult to defend the United States against a surprise attack, along with the number of our enemies and the range of possible targets, is an individualistic and consumer mentality that places a high value on privacy, autonomy, freedom of movement, comfort, and convenience,

and that therefore resents the restrictions on privacy, autonomy, and so forth entailed by effective security measures. This
makes d higher for Americans than for most other peoples; if
we continue to spend heavily on defense against surprise
attacks, it is because the danger of such attacks is also greater
for Americans.

Thus far I have treated d dichotomously: if inequality (1) is
satisfied, the potential victim of a surprise attack should take d
measures; if not, he should take no measures. A more realistic
assumption (which incidentally permits dispensing with b) is
that d can vary. Concretely, if $d = 0$, a is as in inequality (1),
but as d rises, a falls: the more defensive measures that are
taken, the less harm the attack does. The goal, then, in picking
the level of d is to minimize the sum (S) of the expected costs
of the attack and the costs of d, where d is the number of units
of defense and $c(d)$ the cost of defense. Thus

$$S = pa(d) + c(d) + (1-p)w(p, d). \tag{2}$$

S is thus the sum of the costs of false negatives (failing to predict attacks that occur), which is the first term on the right-
hand side of equation (2), and the false positives (false alarms),
which are given by the second and third terms, the second
being the cost of defensive measures and the third the lulling
cost.

Provided that the rate at which an increase in d reduces a
exceeds the rate at which such an increase increases c and w,
S is minimized by taking the derivative of S with respect to d
and setting the result equal to zero, yielding

$$c_d + (1-p)w_d = -pa_d, \tag{3}$$

where a_d is the effect on a (the harm to the victim of the attack)
of a small change in d (the extent of defensive measures), and
c_d and w_d are the effects on c (the cost of defensive measures)

and w (the lulling cost), respectively, also of a small change in d. In words, the optimal expenditure on defensive measures requires increasing them to the point at which a \$1 increase in their cost (including the effect on the lulling cost) reduces the expected cost of the attack by \$1. The greater the effect of such expenditure in reducing the cost of an attack if it occurs, and the higher the probability of an attack (provided the effect on the expected cost of such an attack exceeds the effect on reducing the expected lulling cost), the greater the cost-justified level of measures to anticipate and respond to the attack.

The model is still unrealistic, in being limited to a single prospective surprise attack. A related unrealism is that the model ignores the dynamic character of the crying-wolf phenomenon. The boy who cried wolf did not sound only a single false alarm; it was the repetition of false alarms that made it impossible for him to convince his hearers that his latest alarm was true. In other words, the lulling cost rises with each false alarm.

Assume then that there are t periods in each of which there is an equal probability of an attack that will impose the same costs and cost the same to defend against, and that for every period in which an attack does not occur the lulling cost increases by r percent a year. With this adjustment, the sum of all costs, S in equation (2), becomes

$$S' = tpa(d) + tc(d) + (1 - p)w(d)y(t,p), \qquad (4)$$

where $y(t,p) = t(1 + r)^j$ and j is a probability distribution of p. Notice that y, and hence the lulling cost, increases with t and with r but decreases with p, because the higher p is, the likelier is an attack, and an attack will reduce the lulling cost in the next period. It might, however, replace it with a "hyperalert cost"—a possible increased risk of surprise attack if all attention is focused on preventing a repetition of a previous attack to the neglect of other possible attacks. For example, we may be expending too many resources on screening airline passengers, to the neglect of potential terrorist threats to other parts of the nation's transportation system. In addition, a hyperalert state may precipitate a flood of warnings that turn out to be false alarms (which has certainly been the experience since 9/11), creating new lulling costs. False alarms also draw attention away from true dangers; they are, at best (that is, even without producing a crying-wolf effect), distracting noise. My model ignores all these complications, but they are worth noting to underscore the difficulty of responding intelligently to the threat of surprise attack.

S' is minimized (provided that some plausible restrictions are placed on the terms) when

$$tpc_d = -tpa_d - (1 - p)w_d y(t,p). \tag{5}$$

So, as before, the total investment in defensive measures against a possible surprise attack should be carried to the point at which the cost of an additional measure, plus the increase in expected lulling costs from taking it, would be just equal to the reduction in the expected cost of attacks that the measure would bring about.

The foregoing analysis is offered as a possible aid to identifying relevant considerations and the relations among them. It is not intended as an algorithm. The problem with using a formula to optimize the response to warnings of an attack is the difficulty, bordering on the impossible, of quantifying the terms, other than d and c and in some cases $b(d)$. Assessing the probability of a surprise attack is particularly baffling, as we know. A further difficulty is that a formula cannot be applied across the entire spectrum of possible surprise attacks; this is precluded by the inescapable necessity of filtering data in accordance with the analyst's preconceptions.[33] John Locke and Sherlock Holmes notwithstanding, the mind is not a blank slate. There are a near-infinite number of data points in our visual and auditory fields, and we can't take them all in at once, as Holmes pretends to do.[34] A rational person prioritizes in accordance with his interests. So intelligence officers determine where the greatest dangers lie, and having made that determination give greater weight to incoming information that bears on those dangers than to information on more remote dangers.[35]

This gives rise to the following paradox: a surprise attack is likelier to succeed when it has a low antecedent probability of success and the attacker is weak, because on both counts the victim will discount the danger and because the range of possible low-probability attacks by weak adversaries is much greater than the range of possible high-probability attacks by strong ones. The potential victim marshals his defensive resources to protect the high-probability targets of greatest value, leaving underprotected the immense number of lower-valued low-probability targets. Knowing this, an enemy who wants to achieve strategic surprise picks one of those inferior targets. Realizing that this is what the enemy is likely to do, and that he is therefore unlikely to obtain a decisive victory, the potential victim reckons the expected loss (severity dis-

33. "Cognition cannot be altered by legislation." Betts, note 27 above, at 83.

34. Holmes to Watson: "We approached the case, you remember, with an absolutely blank mind, which is always an advantage. We had formed no theories. We were simply there to observe and to draw inferences from our observations." Arthur Conan Doyle, "The Cardboard Box," in *The New Annotated Sherlock Holmes*, vol. 1, pp. 422, 438 (Leslie S. Klinger, ed., 2004).

35. For a striking demonstration of how people impose strong expectations on their interpretation of sensory data, see Daniel J. Simons and Daniel T. Levin, "Failure to Detect Changes to People during a Real-World Interaction," 5 *Psychonomic Bulletin and Review* 644 (1998).

counted by probability) from the attack as low and so does not invest a great deal in anticipating and taking measures to defend against the attack, especially since the cost of defending against the entire spectrum of low-probability attacks by weak adversaries (who may, moreover, be numerous) is prohibitive.

Surprise attacks are a favorite tactic of the weak[36] because they are a force multiplier, which a weak enemy needs most. When used by the weak they tend to be wild, and ultimately unsuccessful, gambles, but may inflict great damage en route to their ultimate failure.

This may explain why surprise attacks are rare. On the one hand, when employed by the weak, they are indeed gambles, with dim prospects of ultimate success (the weaker of two contenders is likely to lose the contest), and the greater prospect of ultimate defeat is a deterrent. On the other hand, a strong, aggressive state has difficulty achieving strategic surprise because its intentions are anticipated.

The basic elements of this analysis can be formalized with the aid of our original inequality, $pa > (1 - p) d$, which says take defensive measures if but only if the expected cost of an attack exceeds their cost. Assume now that there are two types of attack, one that involves a high probability of inflicting a devastating loss (high p and high a), the other a low probability of inflicting a much smaller loss (low p and low a). Assume further that there are n potential attacks of the first type and n' of the second and that d, the defensive measures necessary to prevent an attack, is the same for each class. Let p' denote the probability of attacks in the second class and a' the harm caused by such an attack, so $p' < p$ and $a' < a$, but $n' > n$.

We now have two inequalities, the first denoting the condition for taking defensive measures against the first type of

36. See, for example, Betts, note 1 above, at 128–138.

attack and the second the condition for taking defensive measures against the second type:

$$n[pa > (1 - p)d] \tag{6a}$$

$$n'[p'a' > (1 - p')d] \tag{6b}$$

The first inequality is much more likely to be satisfied than the second. The fact that there are more potential attacks of the second type is irrelevant. If the expression in brackets is negative, multiplying it, however many times, will not make it positive; and unless it is positive, defensive measures will not be cost justified. The first term in the bracketed expression in inequality (6b), $p'a'$, is smaller than the corresponding term in inequality (6a) because it is the product of two smaller terms, so, for example, if $p = .2$ and $p' = .1$, and $a = 100$ and $a' = 20$, $pa = 20$ and $p'a' = 2$. The second term, $(1 - p')d$, is larger, because d is unchanged but $1 - p'$ is larger than $1 - p$ (in the example, it is .9 versus .8). The smaller the first term and the larger the second, the more likely the bracketed term is to be negative and so the less likely are defensive measures to be justified. In the example, if $d = 5$, the first inequality is $20 - .8(5) = 16$, while the second is $2 - .9(4) = -1.6$. So it does not pay to take defensive measures aimed at averting the lesser attack.

These numbers are arbitrary, but they illustrate how it can be rational to take no defensive measures at all against a large class of potential surprise attacks. This is all the more likely when the costs of information are taken explicitly into account. The existence of those costs—alternatively, the necessity (owing to the limitations of human mental capacity) of economizing on attention[37]—makes it likely that below some thresh-

---

37. Richard A. Posner, *Catastrophe: Risk and Response* 13, 120–122, 169, 182–183 (2004).

old of expected cost, no consideration whatever will be given to taking defensive measures against a class of possible surprise attacks. Such a "threshold heuristic,"[38] which is related to my earlier point about the indispensability of preconceptions to rational thought, may be at once rational and an invitation to attack. It may also be related to an irrational tendency of people to write down small risks to zero,[39] though presumably intelligence professionals and others who deal with risk professionally are less likely to succumb to this tendency than laypeople.

The fundamental problem, however, is the asymmetry of attacker and victim. The attacker picks the time, place, and means of attack. Since without a great deal of luck his plan cannot be discovered in advance by the victim, the attacker has, by virtue of his having the initiative and of the victim's being unable to be strong everywhere all the time, a built-in advantage that assures a reasonable probability of a local success. The Pearl Harbor, Tet (but for its political impact), Yom Kippur, and 9/11 attacks achieved only local successes. But when an attacker is willing to settle for a local success, there is little the victim can do to prevent it.

Finally, as Thomas Schelling has pointed out, the more sensitive a warning system, the greater the risk of the victim's responding mistakenly with a preemptive attack on the supposed attacker. The system "may cause us to identify an attacking plane as a seagull, and do nothing, or it may cause us to identify a seagull as an attacking plane, and provoke our inad-

38. Richard J. Herring, "Credit Risk and Financial Instability," *Oxford Review of Economic Policy*, no. 3, 1999, pp. 63, 71–72; Paul Slovic et al., "Preference for Insuring against Probable Small Losses: Insurance Implications," 44 *Journal of Risk and Insurance* 237, 254–255 (1977).

39. For a comprehensive study, see Howard Kunreuther, *Disaster Insurance Protection: Public Policy Lessons* (1978); Kenneth J. Arrow, "Foreword," in id. at vii.

vertent attack on the enemy."[40] This is still another reason to doubt the wisdom of seeking an airtight defense against surprise attacks.

The analysis in this chapter suggests that surprise attacks cannot reliably be prevented,[41] though some can be, others can be deterred, and the worst consequences of those that do occur can be mitigated, for example by stocking vaccines in anticipation of a possible bioterrorist attack that may not be preventable. Given the nature and tenacity of the obstacles to anticipating and defeating surprise attacks, it would be surprising if a reorganization of the intelligence apparatus could overcome the obstacles—especially a reorganization that creates a more centralized system. The threshold below which attention drops off to zero will be higher the more centralized the intelligence system is. If one person—the Director of National Intelligence—decides which surprise attacks to worry about, the threshold will be very high, because a single individual cannot hold many things in his mind at the same time.

More effective in preventing surprise attacks than reorganizing the intelligence system might be a policy of preventive war designed to preempt surprise attacks. But the objections are formidable (for example, the policy might provoke a preventive attack by an enemy who feared a preventive attack against him), and in any event the suggestion raises issues that are beyond the scope of this book.[42]

---

40. Thomas C. Schelling, *The Strategy of Conflict* 220 (1980 ed.).

41. The general conclusion of the literature on surprise attacks. See, for example, id. at 286–290; Kam, note 1 above, at 213–233.

42. On preventive war generally, see Eric A. Posner and Alan O. Sykes, "Optimal War and Jus ad Bellum" (University of Chicago Law School, Olin Working Paper No. 211, April 2004).

Chapter 4

The Principles
of Intelligence

From the case studies of successful surprise attacks, from my attempt to distill them into a model of the obstacles to anticipating such attacks, and from theories of human action, it may be possible to derive some principles of intelligence. Those principles, when married to the principles of organization, which I take up in the next chapter, may point to the optimal organization of intelligence for foiling surprise attacks.

The goal of intelligence is to learn about the intentions and capabilities of potential enemies (or competitors, in the case of commercial intelligence, but I am not interested in that). Intelligence data are collected by spies, by scrutiny of publicly available ("open source") materials such as newspapers, magazines, the Web, and scientific and technical journals, and by technical means of surveillance, such as imagery (aerial and satellite photography) and signals (electronic surveillance) intelligence. The data are given to analysts to collate and interpret, and the results of their analysis are forwarded to the officials responsible for policy. So there are three levels: *collection*, *analysis*, and *action*, the last being the response to the analysis by the officials who are authorized to act in accordance with what intelligence reveals.[1]

With regard to the collection phase, a standard criticism of U.S. intelligence is that it underuses spies. The reluctance to employ spies is understandable. Spying is a dangerous occupation that attracts more than its share of unsavory and unreliable people. Most spies are nationals of the country spied on and hence traitors, and many spies turn out to be double agents.[2] Betrayal, deception, blackmail, bribery, burglary, and skullduggery seem the very essence of espionage. Thus the crack "Intelligence is the second oldest profession, only with fewer morals." Covert operations, usually intended to obtain or

1. The literature on intelligence is immense. For some highlights (besides works cited in the preceding chapter, notably Roberta Wohlstetter's book), see Robert M. Clarke, *Intelligence Analysis: A Target-Centric Approach* (2004); Abram N. Shulsky and Gary J. Schmitt, *Silent Warfare: Understanding the World of Intelligence* (3d ed., 2002); Gregory F. Treverton, *Reshaping National Intelligence for an Age of Information* (2001); *Agents for Change: Intelligence Services in the 21st Century* (Harold Shukman, ed., 2000); Mark M. Lowenthal, *Intelligence: From Secrets to Policy* (2000); Michael Herman, *Intelligence Power in Peace and War* (1996); Loch K. Johnson, *Secret Agencies: U.S. Intelligence in a Hostile World* (1996); *U.S. Intelligence at the Crossroads: Agendas for Reform* (Roy Godson, Ernest R. May, and Gary Schmitt, eds., 1995); Jeffrey T. Richelson, *A Century of Spies: Intelligence in the Twentieth Century* (1995); Bruce D. Berkowitz and Allan E. Goodman, *Strategic Intelligence for American National Security* (1989). Old but still very worthwhile is Sherman Kent, *Strategic Intelligence for American World Policy* (1949). There are also a number of scholarly journals that specialize in intelligence, such as the *International Journal of Intelligence and CounterIntelligence, Intelligence and National Security*, the *Journal of Intelligence History*, and the *Defense Intelligence Journal*. On "warning intelligence" (intelligence oriented toward detecting a surprise attack, sometimes called "I&W" [Indications and Warnings]), Cynthia M. Grabo, *Anticipating Surprise: Analysis for Strategic Warning* (2002), is particularly good. Lowenthal's book is the best nuts-and-bolts description of the U.S. intelligence system that I know.

2. For example, "we now know that virtually all East German and Cuban spies recruited by the [CIA] were in fact double agents of those states' intelligence services." Abram Shulsky and Gary Schmitt, "Intelligence Reform: Beyond the Ames Case," in *U.S. Intelligence at the Crossroads*, note 1 above, at 47.

exploit intelligence, but in any event conducted by our spy service (the CIA's Directorate of Operations), seem to miscarry or backfire with alarming frequency. Except in time of war, moreover, running spies in foreign countries is a hostile as well as an illegal act directed against a "friendly" nation, and so when a spy is caught the country he is spying for is likely to suffer a diplomatic setback; the State Department's hostility to the CIA is no surprise. Technical means of spying, as by spy satellites, are "cleaner," so it is also no surprise that the United States, which anyway has traditionally concentrated its efforts on the technological side of war, prefers investing in technical than in human espionage and may not be very good at the latter.

Open-source materials are an important source of intelligence. The amount of publicly available information even about closed societies is often considerable (this is true even of terrorist groups, many of which publicize their activities), and the journalists and other producers of such information, including academics, are sometimes better traveled and more highly specialized, and enjoy greater access to target groups, than intelligence professionals. This gives point to Roberta Wohlstetter's observation, quoted in the preceding chapter, that "in comparing the top-secret intelligence evaluations of enemy intentions with estimates in the contemporary press, one is struck by the relative soundness of the less privileged judgments." One reason for this, however, is that the intentions of a potential enemy (especially if it is not, and it usually is not, an open society) are so difficult to discern by *any* method that an intelligence agency may have no advantage over outsiders in guessing at such intentions. Yet the difficulty of gauging enemy capabilities can be as great or even greater[3] — think of

3. Grabo, note 1 above, at 17–24.

how the French underestimated the Germans in 1940, or the Germans the Soviets in 1941, or we the Vietnamese Communists in 1968, or Israel the Egyptians and Syrians in 1973. It is one thing to be able to count the enemy's divisions, aircraft, and other military assets, and another thing to determine how, and how well, they will be used. Predicting and taking effective measures against a surprise attack require being able to gauge *both* intentions and capabilities.

Despite the considerable problems just in collecting intelligence, we know from Chapter 3 that collection is not the most problem-ridden stage of the intelligence process, for there seem always to be plenty of signs of an impending attack. Of course it would be better to have more than a warning sign — to know with certainty the exact date, place, aims, means, and strength of the attack. But it is doubtful that the collection of intelligence data can be improved to a point that would yield such certainty. One reason for doubt, besides the efforts, which are difficult to counter,[4] that an attacker will make to conceal his plans and plant false information, is that he may change the plan of attack at the last moment.

Then too we know that limitations on the resources available for defense, and the impossibility of thinking seriously about an indefinite range of threats, will compel intelligence officers to disregard a host of low-probability events, one of which may turn out to be the surprise attack that does occur. Fear of penetration and leaks makes intelligence officers (and their services) reluctant to share information with each other fully and freely, which in turn makes it difficult to assemble scattered bits of information into a convincing mosaic.[5] The

4. See id., at 120–129, for an excellent discussion of the difficulty of thwarting deception tactics.

5. This reluctance is not only ad hoc; it is codified in the different rules of different intelligence units regarding access to classified information. One

reluctance is rational, and "stovepiping" criticized excessively. Bulkheads in a ship slow movement between the ship's compartments, just as restrictions on sharing classified information slow the communication traffic between intelligence services. But in both cases there is a compelling safety rationale.

Even when intelligence services do share information (which they do to a considerable extent), they are reluctant to identify the sources of the information. Many sources are vulnerable to countermeasures, including spies that the CIA runs in foreign countries, codes of potential enemies that we have broken, and new methods of electronic surveillance that the enemy is unaware of and thus hasn't attempted to neutralize or evade. Yet an analyst who is not told the source of the information that he is being asked to analyze won't know how much weight to give it.[6] The CIA's collectors try to give the analysts a general idea of the reliability of particular intelligence data that they collect, but withhold details that would enable identification of sources. Presumably there is a similar veiling of some of the intelligence obtained by highly secret technical means.

The problem of pooling information is vertical as well as horizontal. Intelligence officers are reluctant to share information about sources with the officials, not themselves intelligence officers, who have to decide what action if any to take on the basis of the information. This reluctance, which is acute because of an understandable concern that politicians, political appointees, and other people outside the intelligence community are more likely to leak sensitive information than intelli-

---

thing that the Intelligence Reform and Terrorism Prevention Act of 2004 did *not* do is empower the Director of National Intelligence to prescribe uniform standards for classification.

6. See Berkowitz and Goodman, note 1 above, at 113–117, for a good discussion of these issues.

gence officers are, can cause the officials to act precipitately, unaware of reliability problems with the information they've been given. This seems to have been a factor in the decision to invade Iraq; the CIA advised the President that Iraq had weapons of mass destruction, but did not disclose the sources of that advice, which were in fact of dubious reliability. (The CIA claims to have communicated its doubts to the action-level officials; I cannot assess the claim.)

The concern with the lulling effect of false alarms is another impediment to the free flow of information about possible attacks. It builds conservatism into warning intelligence. So warning signs tend to be steeply discounted or even suppressed by the intelligence services rather than forwarded to the policymaking level—except in the wake of a surprise attack, when the system becomes hyperalert. Yet that is not a good state to be in either. It means that officials will be flooded with warnings. This may produce a cognitive overload that makes it difficult to sort, prioritize, and respond to the warnings. I mentioned the inescapable need to filter information; the wrinkle here is that filtering is more difficult the more information there is to filter. A state of hyperalertness is also, as I noted in the last chapter, apt to distract an intelligence agency from threats other than the one that has caused it to become hyperalert, though the other threats may be as or more dangerous.

The problems of intelligence analysis that I have mentioned thus far are recognizable as intrinsic to the nature of the task of intelligence without one's having to delve into subtle human factors. Two additional types of problem come into view when those factors are emphasized. I'll call the two types "careerist" and "cognitive." The first term refers to career incentives that put an employee at odds with his employer. My particular concern is with the incentives of intelligence officers who analyze intelligence data that have been collected and forwarded to them and who then forward the results of their analysis to their superiors both within the intelligence service and in the higher reaches of government where action on the basis of intelligence analyses is determined.

I'll start with a contrast: business employees are evaluated, for purposes of assignment, compensation, and promotion, on the basis of the contribution they make to the firm's profits. Uncertainty about that contribution may be acute, especially when employees work in teams, though we'll see that team organization can redeem some of the problems created by that uncertainty. But at least the firm's profits are a known quantity, and they provide a good starting point for evaluating individual employees. In contrast, the output of an intelligence service is difficult to define, let alone quantify.[7] The economics of optimal compensation, itself in an unsatisfactory state,[8] has only limited application to public agencies that produce nonmarket commodities.[9]

Of all such commodities produced by government, intelligence is one of the hardest to value. Given the difficulty of avoiding ever being surprised (not just by attacks—consider how surprised our intelligence services were by the fall of the Shah of Iran, the collapse of Soviet communism, and the Indian

7. Woodrow J. Kuhns, "Intelligence Failures: Forecasting and the Lessons of Epistemology," in *Paradoxes of Strategic Intelligence: Essays in Honor of Michael I. Handel* 80, 82–83 (Richard K. Betts and Thomas G. Mahnken, eds., 2003); Stephen J. Flanagan, "Managing the Intelligence Community," 10 *International Security* 58, 62 (1985).

8. For excellent discussions, see Joseph E. Stiglitz, "Incentives, Information, and Organization Design, 16 *Empirica* 3 (1989); George P. Baker, Michael C. Jensen, and Kevin J. Murphy, "Compensation and Incentives: Practice vs. Theory," 43 *Journal of Finance* 593 (1988).

9. Avinash Dixit, "Incentives and Organizations in the Public Sector: An Interpretive Review," 37 *Journal of Human Resources* 696 (2002).

and Pakistani nuclear-weapons tests), it would be as absurd to set the benchmark of satisfactory performance at anticipating 100 percent of surprises as it would be to define a good batting percentage in major-league baseball as 1.000, or for that matter .500. Even to think in percentage terms when evaluating intelligence officers could have perverse incentive effects, since one way never to be caught unawares is to list every possible attack and "warn" that any one of them may occur tomorrow, the day after tomorrow, and so on till the end of time. That kind of intelligence product, though in a sense accurate (but only in the sense in which a stopped clock is accurate twice a day), would be worthless.

The absence of a benchmark not only makes it difficult to evaluate the performance of intelligence officers; it also makes it difficult for an intelligence service to fend off unjust accusations of failure. When a batter who bats .333 strikes out, we don't say he "failed" (unless perhaps it is a crucial game), because we know that it requires outstanding skill to achieve a ratio of one hit to two outs. But every surprise that an intelligence service does not anticipate is counted a "failure," because no one has any idea of what a good batting average in intelligence is.

It would not be realistic to expect an intelligence service to be able to compile—what effective prevention of surprise attacks would require—a list of possible attacks with time-specific probability estimates for each (a 10 percent probability of Attack A this week, 20 percent next week, a 5 percent probability of Attack B this week, 15 percent next week, etc.). Even if an intelligence service could do this, the accuracy of its estimates could not be verified. If an attack occurred that the service had estimated to have only a 1 percent chance of occurring, that would not prove the service right; and if defensive measures were taken to stave off a surprise attack that the service had thought 99 percent likely to occur if those measures were not taken, and the attack did not occur, this would not prove that the 99 percent estimate was right, either.

About the best one can hope for, though it may be impossible to discover whether the hope has been fulfilled, is that an intelligence service be able to anticipate "most" surprise attacks, especially the most lethal ones, with the "fewest" false alarms—a vital qualification because of the lulling cost that I emphasized in the last chapter and the sheer cognitive overload produced by a flood of alarms. And yet a very high ratio of true to false alarms is not an acceptable measure of an intelligence service's success, because it is consistent with a very high rate of failing to give true alarms. An intelligence officer who in his entire career predicted only one attack, and that a real one, would have an infinite ratio of true to false alarms (1/0), yet might have failed to predict other surprise attacks that had occurred and that a less fastidious analyst would have predicted. The goal of "warning intelligence," as we saw in the last chapter, should be to minimize the sum of the costs of false negatives (failing to predict an attack that occurs) and the costs of false positives (false alarms), and not just one or the other. But we also saw that it is impossible to specify with any precision the degree of cost minimization that is feasible and so would provide a rational benchmark for evaluating an intelligence service's performance.

With the output of an intelligence service so difficult to value, measuring the performance of the individual intelligence officers or executives who are responsible for deciding when to warn higher officials of an impending attack is a baffling undertaking indeed. And whenever it is very difficult to evaluate employees' performance, a space is opened in which they can pursue self-interested objectives at the expense of the employer, and, being self-interested human beings, they are likely to do so. (Economists discuss this problem under the aegis of "agency costs"—the costs resulting from the inability of the principal to fully align the agent's incentives with his own.)[10] Specifically, one can expect intelligence officers to protect their jobs by (1) avoiding definite predictions, (2) erring on the side of not sounding the alarm,[11] (3) deferring the making of a prediction, while gathering more information, (4) hesitating to update predictions on the basis of new information, (5) shying away from making predictions that are inconsistent with what their colleagues and superiors are predicting, and (6), in the wake of an attack, overemphasizing intelligence directed at preventing an exact repetition of it. This list is not intended to impugn anyone's patriotism; the behaviors that I am calling careerist are largely unconscious and may be less common than in other fields in which it is difficult to monitor employees' performance.

The reason for point 1 is that, as I noted earlier, the more precise a prediction is, the likelier it is to be wrong. An intelligence officer is much more likely to be correct in predicting a terrorist attack on the United States in the next year than in the next 48 hours. But the less precise the prediction, the less value it has.

Point 3, the tendency to call for more information before acting on a warning of an impending attack,[12] backs up point

10. But who exactly *is* the principal, in the case of public employees? See generally Anthony Downs, *Inside Bureaucracy* 77–78 (1967). The modern literature is illustrated, again in the context of organizations, though business rather than government, by Philippe Aghion and Jean Tirole, "Formal and Real Authority in Organizations," 105 *Journal of Political Economy* 1 (1997).

11. "The true professional will under-warn, even to the point that the recipient will have to read between the lines or ask for further information to realize that he is being warned at all." Grabo, note 1 above, at 167.

12. See, for example, David E. Sanger and David Johnston, "Bin Laden Tape Unsettled President's Aides," *New York Times* (national ed.), Nov. 6, 2004, p.

2, the tendency to underwarn: "it is usually safer to fail to predict something which does happen than to make a positive prediction that something will happen and it does not. In the first case, it can always be maintained that there was insufficient evidence to come to a positive judgment."[13] Calling for more information also sounds reassuringly prudent and postpones the put-up-or-shut-up day on which the analyst will have to make a definite prediction that is therefore likely to be incorrect. The more information the analyst acquires, moreover, the likelier he is (within limits—an important qualification explored below) to be able to make a correct prediction. Should a surprise attack occur while the additional information is being hunted down, the analyst may be criticized. But he can defend himself by pointing to the danger of basing costly or provocative countermeasures on incomplete information that turns out to be mistaken, as in the case of our preemptive invasion of Iraq. The cost of false alarms induces a general reluctance to sound the alarm because it is impossible to know in advance whether the alarm will be true or false.

Point 4 (conservatism in updating) reflects the fact that changing one's prediction on the basis of new information is likely to be read as an acknowledgment that the previous prediction was erroneous, though it may actually have been the most accurate prediction possible given the limited information then available. As for point 5 (reluctance to take a lone stand), if an officer makes a prediction that is contrary to the office consensus, and he is wrong, he will be blamed. But if he goes along with the consensus, and the consensus is wrong, the blame will be diffused. Point 6 is rather similar. After an attack occurs, the highest priority will tend to be given to preventing

---

A9, explaining that no increase in the alert status was ordered because some officials "wanted a more detailed analysis of the tape."

13. Grabo, note 1 above, at 168–169.

an exact repetition of that attack, even if different kinds of attack carry a higher expected cost, as may well be true since 9/11; terrorist attacks that would not involve airplanes could do much greater harm. But should the exact attack be repeated, the failure of the intelligence system to have anticipated it would be regarded as irrefutable proof of complete incompetence, and many heads would roll. In addition, it is easier to design an effective measure to deal with a known event; that design can be offered as evidence that the intelligence system has fixed the problem. Closing the barn door after the horses have escaped doesn't do any good, but at least it is a decisive action.

Point 2, the tendency to underwarn, is due principally to the fact that false alarms are potentially much more common than true ones because of the inherent ambiguity of warning signs. The warning signs that U.S. intelligence officers received before Pearl Harbor were consistent with a wide variety of Japanese moves over a considerable interval of time. A vast number of equiprobable predictions could have been made on the basis of the warning signs, and since the Japanese could launch only a handful of surprise attacks, most of the predictions would have been falsified by events. An intelligence officer who was forever warning of an impending attack would generate a very high ratio of false to true positives. Richard Clarke, we know from Chapter 1, suffered a career setback by obsessively warning that there would be a serious attack by al Qaeda. When the attack finally came, which might have been regarded as vindication, he received no praise for his prescience, because by being right he had made his superiors look bad, and because he had, knowing what he knew, failed to prevent the attack. A related point, particularly applicable to the CIA, is that one form a response to a warning may take is directing an intelligence agency to conduct a risky operation, which if it fails may end the careers of some of the agency's employees.[14]

Surprise attacks are low-probability events and thus tend to occur at long intervals. Careers are finite, and this increases the asymmetry of career rewards for predicting that a surprise attack will happen and predicting that it will not happen. A prediction of a surprise attack may be correct, but if the attack does not materialize until the officer who made the prediction has retired, he will get no reward for his prescience. If he predicts that there will be no surprise attack, which is anyway the prediction usually preferred by the officials responsible for acting (or not acting) in response to intelligence, because it excuses them from having to act, he will not be punished should the attack occur after his retirement.

Once an attack occurs, however, the tendency to underwarn is suspended and even reversed. Now everyone is hyperalert. In the wake of the post-9/11 investigations by Congress and the 9/11 Commission, no intelligence officer wants to be the needle in the haystack that an investigative body finds after the next attack and blames for the failure to thwart it. No longer (for the time being, anyway) is the greater career risk being a Chicken Little pestering one's superiors with prophecies of doom that never materialize; instead it is failing to report every warning sign to one's superiors, even if the result is to bury them in unfiltered and inconsistent warnings.

But every month that goes by without an attack on the United States saps the alertness of the intelligence services. The growing interval nurtures hopes that the greatest danger is past; physical and mental fatigue and sheer boredom turn hopes into wishful thinking. If alertness does remain high,

14. Anonymous [Michael Scheuer], *Imperial Hubris: Why the West Is Losing the War on Terror* 238 (2004).

moreover, it may, as I pointed out in the last chapter, distract the intelligence system from threats that may be greater than the one that caused the system to become alert. In the long run, this problem can be overcome by expanding the system so that it can attend to the other threats without reducing the resources allocated to what is thought to be the greatest threat. But expansion takes time, may be a budget buster, and by making the system larger may make it more unwieldy.

The problem of lagged response is serious because of the difficulty that I noted in Chapter 1 of getting people worried about mere future threats. When the Cold War ended and a Democratic President was elected who was not much interested in national security affairs (and would not have been elected had the Cold War not ended), the controversial side of the CIA—namely the clandestine service—was cut back. The 9/11 attacks, and the Iraq WMD fiasco, indicated that the cutback had gone too far; but it takes time to produce intelligence officers with the requisite training, experience, and foreign-language proficiency.

Besides the propensity of intelligence analysts to make vague and optimistic predictions, effective analysis is impeded by the analysts' reluctance to share with others the information on which they are planning to base their predictions, especially if those others work for rival bureaus. This tendency should be distinguished from the service's own concern with preventing leakage and penetration, a concern based on the fact that disclosing the identity of sources (whether human or technical, including code-breaking) may enable an enemy to neutralize them. This unavoidable stumbling block to effective analysis looms particularly large when the intelligence service, having completed its analysis, forwards its results to action-level officials; for the danger of leaks is greater at that level. But here I wish to note the career incentives to sequester information.

Information is the most valuable commodity that an intelligence officer possesses. He cannot sell it to other officers or bureaus—he has no intellectual property right—and if he gives the information away "free," the person or service he gives it to is likely to get credit for any success that the information enables; if the recipient is a fellow officer he may use the information to advance his own career at the expense of the officer who gave it to him. Another way to put this is that in the intelligence business, information is power, and people are reluctant to surrender power. With information that no one else has (and thus can act on), you have a bit of control over the future; and you will be tempted to hold back the information to try to shape the future.

The best strategy for an intelligence officer who has a valuable piece of intelligence may be either to use it to provide, without disclosing it, a better analysis than his rivals (or, to the same end, to hoard it while awaiting receipt of additional information to pool it with), or to swap it for other intelligence. The former course of action (hiding) impedes the pooling of information, and the latter is slow and uncertain because barter is an inefficient mode of transacting and because people with good analytic skills but little information (an intelligence analyst, for example) will have little to trade. In addition, pride in one's own service, which is important to esprit de corps, may lead intelligence officers to exaggerate the indiscretion of members of rival bureaus, or of officials who are not part of the intelligence "community," as it is called (misleadingly, since the ethos is competitive rather than communitarian).

Reluctance to share information is common in business firms as well as in intelligence agencies. A worker who shares his know-how with other workers, especially young workers paid lower salaries, may find that he has shared himself out of a job. One way in which a firm can try to overcome its workers' reluctance to share their know-how with each other is by basing wages on team performance. For then the wage of each member of the team depends on that performance and so all the members have an incentive to pool their knowledge; all benefit. But this works only in small teams; in large ones the incentive to cooperate to maximize the value of the team's output is offset by the incentive to shirk when one's own contribution to the team is likely to have only a slight effect on that output. There is no way in which the U.S. intelligence community, with its tens of thousands of employees, can be organized as a single team, and anyway valuing the output of an intelligence team is as difficult as valuing the output of an individual intelligence officer. Intelligence officers do of course work together, even across agency lines, but it is doubtful that greater emphasis on team production of intelligence would significantly increase quality.

The interaction between intelligence officers and officials at the action level introduces additional careerist obstacles. Because of the uncertainties inherent in intelligence and the fact that so much of it derives from open sources, such as newspapers and television, to which action-level officials have the same access as intelligence officers, those officials are likely to have their own ideas about the various threats that the nation may be facing.[15] They also have their own sources of private information, such as conversations with their foreign counterparts, that they may be reluctant to share with their intelligence

15. Berkowitz and Goodman, note 1 above, at 107–108; Treverton, note 1 above, at 145–147. "Perhaps this is revealing a certain arrogance on my part, but I frequently think I am as capable of coming up with an informed opinion about a matter as any number of the people within the Intelligence Community who feel that they have been uniquely anointed with this responsibility." Paul Wolfowitz, "Comment," in *U.S. Intelligence at the Crossroads*, note 1 above, at 75, 76. Wolfowitz when he made this remark had recently completed a stint as Undersecretary of Defense for Policy.

services. They may be tenacious in adhering to their own intelligence ideas and irritated to be challenged by the intelligence bureaucracy, especially if like many high officials they regard most civil servants as drones and time servers of dubious loyalty to their (temporary) superiors. The officials may be looking to the intelligence service to validate and support their own independent estimates; knowing this, career-minded intelligence officers may bend their predictions to conform to their superiors' preconceptions.[16]

The tendency of officials at the policymaking level to be their own intelligence officers is reinforced by a rational distrust of intelligence professionals that is based on the known reluctance of civil servants, even those not involved with classified materials, to share information with their superiors, especially with short-termers brought in from the private sector who just serve for a year or two and so start out with a knowledge deficit that a canny civil servant will do his best to preserve. The civil servant's reluctance to be candid with his superiors is rational. The better informed the superior is, the easier it is for him to challenge the advice he receives from his subordinates. Realizing this, they will be chary about conveying information to their superior, who, aware of this tendency, will tend to discount the advice he receives from his subordinates and to turn elsewhere for guidance. The longer the ladder of command—and the Intelligence Reform Act has lengthened it by slotting in the Director of National Intelligence above the CIA director and the other heads of intelligence services and thus far above the actual intelligence collectors and analysts—the less information will reach the top.

The career tensions between intelligence professionals and

16. Gerald W. Hopple, "Intelligence and Warning: Implications and Lessons of the Falkland Islands War," 36 *World Politics* 339, 342–343 (1984).

their political superiors are aggravated by politics. Democrats tend to be distrustful of the national security apparatus—particularly the CIA, a traditional liberals' bugaboo—and Republicans tend to be distrustful of civil servants, most of whom, they assume, are closet liberals.

Thus far in discussing the tension between the intelligence professionals and their political superiors, while I have mentioned politics I have not discussed the politicization of intelligence itself. But that is a serious problem too. A President's reasons for action may be politically motivated, in the sense of being related to his political fortunes and ambitions, and his party loyalties, rather than to his sense of what is the soundest policy. (Of course he may confuse his political interests with the public interest.) If determined upon a risky course, he will want the backing of the intelligence community. That will be more easily obtained the more centralized the intelligence system is. In the system as it existed before the Intelligence Reform Act, the director of the CIA—the intelligence official most directly subject to Presidential pressure—was only one of the nation's senior intelligence officials and could not speak for the entire intelligence community. Others could disagree and he could use their disagreement to deflect the Presidential wrath if he himself also disagreed with the President. Under the new system, with its concentration of unprecedented power in the Director of National Intelligence, the other senior intelligence officials will be less influential; the President will have only one mind in the intelligence community to bend to his will.

The careerist impediments to reliable (and, as we have just been seeing, relied on) intelligence analysis are reinforced by cognitive limitations. The most important of these, noted in Chapter 3, is the mind's inability to process all the data presented to it by the senses. The data are too voluminous. What is actually seen and heard, in the sense of *usable* inputs into thought and eventually action, is a product of preselection, of preconceptions. The information collected and forwarded to the intelligence analyst and used by him in making predictions will be selected, shaped, and interpreted in light of expectations. Those expectations will have been formed by a variety of factors, including previous intelligence reports, and will operate as a filter for new data. The greater the flow of incoming data, the bigger will be the effect of preconceptions on the response to data because the greater will be the need for filtering to stem the flood. That is one reason analysts who limit themselves to open-source materials sometimes make better predictions than professional intelligence analysts swamped with secret data. More can be less.

There is nothing irrational about the phenomenon of preselection or filtering; it is a rational adjustment to the limited information-processing capacity of the human mind. Similarly, the "economy of attention"—the inability of the human mind to hold in it an indefinite number of subjects, which may drive the intelligence analyst to concentrate on the higher-probability risks and write down the lower-probability ones to zero—is rational, given the mind's limitations. Yet we know that it is from the set of low-probability risks that surprise attacks are most likely to be drawn. Richard Clarke annoyed his superiors in the Bush administration by his preoccupation with al Qaeda because they were focused on other threats that they considered, incorrectly but not necessarily irrationally, to be more serious. They didn't have time to worry about everything, and the terrorist threat was one of the things they placed on the back burner. Prioritization on the basis of expected costs is quintessentially rational. But when probabilities cannot be estimated even roughly, the result of prioritization is unlikely to be satisfactory and may indeed be arbitrary—and this apart from the fact that, as we saw in the last chapter, ranking dangers by their probability may systematically push surprise attacks below the intelligence horizon.

The effect of cognitive limitations in causing erroneous judgments is the subject of a large literature in cognitive psychology,[17] some of it highly relevant to the intelligence business. In the case of market activities, where a great premium is placed on rational decision making, specifically on rational profit maximization, there is both a strong motivation to weed out employees who cannot make rational judgments concerning the tasks they are assigned and monetary penalties for not thinking rationally and, by such lapses, reducing the firm's profits. The market antidotes to irrationality are imperfect—for example, they apparently don't immunize securities analysts, the counterparts in financial markets to intelligence analysts, against cognitive distortions.[18] Intelligence analysis is a nonmarket activity, so we should expect cognitive distortions to be especially common there. One distortion is wishful thinking, which has played a role in many intelligence failures, such as Pearl Harbor. Officials responsible for taking action based on intelligence reports naturally are prone to underestimate the need for taking risky or otherwise costly actions. The intelligence analyst himself, a step down from the action officials, doesn't have to worry directly about the difficulty of heading off any surprise attack that he predicts. But if his intelligence

17. See, for example, *Heuristics and Biases: The Psychology of Intuitive Judgment* (Thomas Gilovich, Dale Griffin, and Daniel Kahneman, eds., 2002).

18. See, for example, Werner F. M. De Bondt and Richard H. Thaler, "Do Analysts Overreact?" in id. at 678; Kent Daniel, David Hirshleifer, and Siew Hong Teoh, "Investor Psychology in Capital Markets: Evidence and Policy Implications," 49 *Journal of Management Economics* 139, 147–149 (2002); Ashiq Ali, April Klein, and James Rosenfeld, "Analysts' Use of Information about Permanent and Transitory Earnings Components in Forecasting Annual EPS," 67 *Accounting Review* 183 (1992).

service is under pressure from the action-level officials to make predictions that support those officials' expectations, their wishful thinking may seep down into his estimates.

Another cognitive distortion arises from the difficulty people have in taking seriously dangers that have never before materialized.[19] It is related to what cognitive psychologists call the availability heuristic[20]—the tendency to give undue weight to information that stands out strongly—and more basically to the cost of thinking, because people find it easier to think about uncertain events in terms of frequencies than of probabilities.[21] A frequency implies that something has happened more than once in the past and so may well occur about as often in the future; it is the basis of inductive reasoning. A probability may be attached to something that has never happened but might yet, and probabilities lacking an anchor in previous experience tend not be taken seriously. So what has happened has greater influence on planning for the future than what may happen; hence the joke about generals always preparing to fight the last war.

It is no accident that the 9/11 Commission's report is mainly concerned with how to prevent a more or less identical repetition of the 9/11 attacks—not only because they actually happened but also because their dramatic and horrifying character gave them unusual salience—to the neglect of even more ominous possibilities that have not yet materialized, such as a man-made smallpox epidemic or a nuclear attack, maybe ship-

19. This is a major focus of my book *Catastrophe: Risk and Response* (2004).

20. See, for example, Norbert Schwarz and Leigh Ann Vaughn, "The Availability Heuristic Revisited: Ease of Recall and Content of Recall as Distinct Sources of Information," in *Heuristics and Biases*, note 17 above, at 103.

21. Posner, note 19 above, at 10, and references in id. at 270 nn. 20–21. The availability heuristic can be understood in similar terms: imagination cost, a component of the cost of thinking, is minimized by a vivid, dramatic event; hence the salience of such events in our thinking.

borne, by a terrorist gang that has managed to steal or build an atomic bomb. The tendency is likely to afflict intelligence services. It is also an impediment to maintaining a political commitment to adequate support of those services, because the probability of a future attack tends not to impress people as a real danger. As memory of the 9/11 attacks fades (it has already faded to some extent), political support for warning intelligence and other defensive measures will wane.[22]

The failure to prevent the 9/11 attacks was due not to their being unimaginable—for they were imaginable and imagined—but to the fact that the imaginable covers too broad a surface, which is one reason for focusing on things that have happened before; the set of bad things that have never happened but may happen in the future is well-nigh infinite. And the more information, including imaginative conjectures covering the full range of the possible, that is clamoring for the mind's attention, the harder it is for the analyst to sift the information for clues—a central finding in Wohlstetter's study of the Pearl Harbor disaster.[23] Hence the "threshold heuristic" that I mentioned in the last chapter.

Another cognitive tendency that Wohlstetter's study flags has come to be known as "mirror imaging":[24] attributing to the leaders of a foreign nation or group the same basic knowledge, reasoning processes, psychology, and values as one's own. This is natural behavior because our ability to navigate the social world depends on assuming that the people we deal with are much like us, and in particular react to things as we do; oth-

22. Paul R. Pillar, "Counterterrorism after Al Qaeda," 27 *Washington Quarterly* 101 (2004).

23. See also Steve Chan, "The Intelligence of Stupidity: Understanding Failures in Strategic Warning," 73 *American Political Science Review* 171, 175 (1979).

24. Lowenthal, note 1 above, at 80–81.

erwise we would find it extremely difficult to coordinate our behavior with theirs. This works fine in our own group, which ordinarily is all that's required, but because we are as a result habituated to thinking this way, we find it difficult to accept more than notionally the possibility of truly alien modes of thought.

There is also the well-known, but not easily avoidable, danger of group thinking.[25] A committee or other collectivity is likely to push toward consensus in order to save time by heading off wrangling and also to maintain friendly relations. But finding oneself in a group of like-thinking individuals is likely to induce complacency and a stubborn resistance to challenges to the consensus; one is fortified in one's beliefs (which may be erroneous) by the fact that they are shared by one's peers. The reluctance to acknowledge one's mistakes is a related point, illustrating the cognitive distortions that arise from the social effects (effects on promotion, for example) of one's beliefs. That reluctance is also related to my earlier point that preconceptions shape our interpretation of new data. The result is "confirmation bias," a tendency to interpret new data as supporting one's priors,[26] leading in turn to "excessive conservatism in belief revision."[27] There is also the simple psychological point, which reinforces careerist reluctance to share information, that the emphasis that intelligence services naturally place on secrecy develops in their officers "a deeply ingrained passion for secrecy."[28]

25. Irving L. Janis, *Groupthink: Psychological Studies of Policy Decisions and Fiascoes* (1982).

26. Matthew Rabin, "Psychology and Economics," 36 *Journal of Economic Literature* 11, 26–28 (1998), and references cited there.

27. Philip L. Tetlock, "Theory-Driven Reasoning about Plausible Pasts and Probable Futures in World Politics," in *Heuristics and Biases*, note 17 above, at 749, 761.

28. David Boren et al., "Guiding Principles for Intelligence Reform," 150 Cong. Rec. S9428 (Sept. 21, 2004).

All these points converge on the proposition that "in general, the value of information is likely to be lower if people behave as cognitive theory claims rather than according to traditional decision theory [i.e., rational cost-benefit analysis]."[29] This is an ominous observation in the context of intelligence reform, since information is the commodity in which intelligence deals.

Deferring to the next chapter a consideration of possible organizational solutions to the problems of intelligence discussed here, let us consider how other types of measure might alleviate them, apart from the obvious ones—better screening of applicants for intelligence jobs, higher salaries to attract better people, ampler resources for technical means of surveillance, better language training, less squeamishness about the selection and control of spies, more respectful consideration of the views of journalists, academics, and other outsiders to the intelligence profession, better education of high officials in the nature and limitations of intelligence, and (as already accomplished, however, by the USA PATRIOT Act) eliminating artificial barriers to the pooling of intelligence data.

Several slightly less obvious possibilities may merit consideration as well. One is a greater investment in research in artificial intelligence, in the hope of developing systems that would enable computers to analyze the vast amounts of intelligence data collected by the intelligence services, without the cognitive distortions that are peculiar to the human mind; we need not fear a computer's succumbing to wishful thinking, group thinking, or confirmation bias. A second possibility is more-generous early retirement benefits (although they are already

29. Roger C. Noll and James E. Krier, "Some Implications of Cognitive Psychology for Risk Regulation," 19 *Journal of Legal Studies* 747, 764 (1990).

pretty generous). These would be intended to make intelligence officers intellectually bolder by enhancing their opportunities for a second career should their boldness truncate their career in intelligence. But I admit that this measure would also exacerbate the asymmetry I noted earlier in the rewards for optimistic versus pessimistic predictions of low-probability events. An alternative might be to strengthen the employment protections that intelligence officers enjoy; in other words, to give them some approximation to tenure in recognition that the difficulty of evaluating their output makes their jobs insecure and by doing so may induce excessive caution.

Another possibility would be a selective relaxation in civil liberties protections that inhibit intelligence gathering and analysis. Still another would be to alter the promotion ladder in the intelligence services to deemphasize managerial potential. The way you rise in the intelligence services now is by being promoted into the ranks of management. But the skills of an analyst and of a manager are different. The analyst angling for promotion may err on the side of caution in his predictions because "wild men" tend not to make good managers. A good salesman is rewarded by being generously compensated, not by being made a manager, unless he happens to have outstanding managerial skills. He may be paid more than his manager, just as a professor may be paid more than his dean. The intelligence services might likewise benefit from decoupling salary from managerial rank.

A measure for improving intelligence analysis that is regularly proposed and as regularly derided is to assign some intelligence officers to be devil's advocates, who would challenge their service's consensus and by doing so shake up preconceptions and combat tendencies to wishful thinking, group thinking, and the underestimation of novel dangers.[30] It may

30. The Intelligence Reform Act has a characteristically ambiguous provi-

well be a bad idea.[31] The best officers will be reluctant to volunteer for an assignment that may impede their promotion prospects by setting them at odds with their colleagues. Those who are appointed will for the same reason tend to pull their punches; no one who seeks advancement in a government bureaucracy wants to be known as a maverick. A consensus may actually be strengthened by a challenge from a devil's advocate, even if it's a vigorous challenge (perhaps especially if it's vigorous), because people become defensive when challenged and because beating back the challenge will, like any victory, induce complacence. An attempt to avoid this problem by allowing the devil's advocate to present his conclusions to the policymaking or action-taking officials would be likely to founder on the officials' desire for crisp advice, stemming from their inability to umpire a debate between specialists. In short, "co-ordinating all-source information in a form which makes it accessible to and usable by policy-makers, while at the same time giving appropriate weight to dissenting opinions, is the intelligence equivalent of squaring the circle."[32]

The prospects for dramatically improving the ability of the intelligence system to anticipate surprise attacks are dim. The

---

sion concerning the matter: "The Director of National Intelligence shall establish a process and assign an individual or entity the responsibility for ensuring that, as appropriate, elements of the intelligence community conduct alternative analysis (commonly referred to as 'red-team analysis') of the information and conclusions in intelligence products." Intelligence Reform and Terrorism Prevention Act of 2004, Title I, § 1017(a). The ambiguity is created by the phrase "as appropriate."

31. This is not to question the value of using "red teams" in the planning of operations. It is an intrinsic feature of any war gaming—you must be playing against an opponent. This is not the sense in which the Intelligence Reform Act refers to "red-team analysis" in the passage quoted in the preceding footnote.

32. Christopher Andrew, "Intelligence in the Cold War: Lessons and Learning," in *Agents for Change*, note 1 above, at 1, 12.

difficulties are multiple and deeply rooted.[33] So destructive can such attacks be that if the difficulties involved in anticipating them could be overcome they would have been overcome by now. I have mentioned some modest possibilities for improvement. But the most critical factors in the success of an intelligence system, at least on the basis of the analysis conducted thus far, appear to be the quality of the management of the intelligence services and the quality of the President and other high officials who must decide on the basis of the intelligence reports they receive how to respond to the threat of a surprise attack. The qualities that enable a person to ascend to the U.S. Presidency are unlikely to include a talent for evaluating the information presented in briefings by intelligence officials. (President Eisenhower and the first President Bush—a former Director of Central Intelligence—are the only exceptions that come to mind.) Other officials at the policymaking level of government tend likewise to be birds of passage, slotted in above the career intelligence officers for a few years. Overworked generalists, confident (often overconfident) of their decision-making competence, they are distrustful of the information they receive from the intelligence services—especially if they understand the cognitive limitations and career concerns that beset intelligence officers.

33. In like vein, an article on disasters lists the following common causes of "large-scale intelligence failures": "rigidities in institutional beliefs, distracting decoy phenomena, neglect of outside complaints, multiple information-handling difficulties, exacerbation of the hazards by strangers, failure to comply with regulations, and a tendency to minimize emergent danger." Barry A. Turner, "The Organizational and Interorganizational Development of Disasters," 21 *Administrative Science Quarterly* 378 (1976). Even nature's "surprise attacks" have a generic resemblance to the pattern illustrated by Pearl Harbor and 9/11. See, for example, the following excellent early account of the December 2004 Indian Ocean tsunami: Kate Linebaugh et al., "Why Quake Warnings Failed: Hours after Indonesia Was Hit, Victims in Africa Had No Inkling," *Wall Street Journal*, Dec. 29, 2004, p. B1.

Chapter 5

The Principles
of Organization

Having examined the phenomenon of the successful surprise attack and the inherent difficulties (epistemic, psychological, political, bureaucratic) that explain why such attacks so often succeed, I now consider whether some of these difficulties might be overcome by reorganizing our intelligence system, the focus of the 9/11 Commission's recommendations and of their legislative implementation. The proper note to sound at the outset is a pessimistic one. As noted in Chapter 1, the failure to anticipate the 9/11 attacks does not seem attributable to the way in which the U.S. intelligence system is organized; nor have the subsequent chapters uncovered evidence that organization was the culprit.

A reorganization is a questionable response to a problem that is not a problem of organization. This banal point tends to be overlooked because organizational changes are often easier and cheaper to make than other reforms, as they may amount to little more than changing job titles and redrawing a table of organization. At the same time they are highly visible—even dramatic—measures and thus convey the impression, however misleading, of a vigorous response to an organization's failure, even if it is not an organizational failure. "Efforts at comprehensive administrative reorganization, like other governmental programs, are symbols of the possibility of meaningful action. Confessions of impotence are not acceptable; leaders are expected to act, and reorganizations provide an opportunity to symbolize action. Presidents who promise reforms apparently do not suffer if they fail to implement them. Announcing a major reorganization symbolizes the possibility of effective leadership, and the belief in that possibility may be of greater significance than the execution of it."[1] We observed in Part I of this book the determination of the 9/11 Commission to achieve a legislative success; how better to assure such a success than to propose an organizational solution to the problem of intelligence failure?

Such a solution can be costly even if the new organization is no worse than the old one. A reorganization may not be costly in financial terms, but it is likely to impose substantial nonpecuniary costs, if only because of the disruption of work routines and lines of command that is bound to accompany the transition to a new organization. Often years will be required to restore the agency's performance to its level before the reorganization. In a report on the newly formed Department of Homeland Security, the General Accounting Office noted that "generally, successful transformations of large organizations, even those undertaking less strenuous reorganizations and with less pressure for immediate results, can take from 5 to 7 years to achieve."[2] That department is only two years old, yet

1. James G. March and Johan P. Olson, "Organizing Political Life: What Administrative Reorganization Tells Us about Government," 77 *American Political Science Review* 281, 290 (1983) (citations omitted).

2. United States General Accounting Office, "Major Management Challenges and Program Risks: Department of Homeland Security" 4 (GAO-03-102, Jan. 2003). Recall from the Introduction the criticisms of the department. One of the critical articles, Eli Lehrer, "The Homeland Security Bureaucracy," *Pub-*

already a distinguished panel has concluded that "the current organization of DHS must be reformed because it hampers the Secretary of Homeland Security's ability to lead our nation's homeland security efforts. The organization is weighted down with bureaucratic layers, is rife with turf warfare, and lacks a structure for strategic thinking and policymaking . . . The department has been slow to overcome the obstacles to becoming an effective 21st century national security instrument."[3] Will we be reading a similar assessment of our reorganized intelligence system two years from now? Are we at the beginning of an era of incessant, restless tinkering with the organization of the system? It is small comfort that the intelligence system has fewer employees than the Department of Homeland Security. It has enough—tens of thousands, scattered among 15 agencies (compared to 22 for DHS)[4]—and its budget is as large as or larger than the department's. The intelligence budget is classified but is estimated to be about $40 billion; the department's is roughly the same.

The problem of transition-induced dysfunction was overlooked by the chairman of the 9/11 Commission in his repeated public warnings that if consideration of the commission's proposals were deferred until Congress reconvened in January

---

lic Interest, summer 2004, pp. 71, 72, aptly notes "the checkered history of American bureaucratic reform."

3. David Heyman and James Jay Carafano, "DHS 2.0: Rethinking the Department of Homeland Security" 7 (Center for Strategic and International Studies and Heritage Foundation, Dec. 13, 2004).

4. The total number of employees engaged in intelligence other than tactical military intelligence, and therefore "under" the DNI in some sense, is classified but probably exceeds 100,000. The CIA is estimated to have about 20,000 employees and the National Security Agency (the largest of the intelligence agencies) about 30,000. Dana Milbank, "Goss Backed '95 Bill to Slash Intelligence: Plan Would Have Cut Personnel 20%," *Washington Post*, Aug. 24, 2004, p. A3; Eric Rosenberg, "Rumsfeld Anchors the Line against Intelligence Czar," *Pittsburgh Post-Gazette*, Aug. 22, 2004, p. A4.

2005, legislation adopting the proposals might come too late to avert a repetition of the 9/11 attacks. On the contrary, adoption of the proposals was bound to usher in a protracted period of increased vulnerability to attack by dislocating the intelligence system. Lines of communication would be disrupted, jobs shuffled, employees unsettled and jockeying for position, turf warfare intensified—ideal conditions for the attacker.

An even greater danger looms: if the public believes that Congress has fixed the intelligence system, investment in alternative methods of protecting the nation will lose support and wither. (This is another example of lulling costs.) Intelligence can be oversold—that is an implication of the analysis in the preceding two chapters. It is an important part of an all-around system of national security, but only a part. It cannot do the job by itself because no feasible changes in the structure, personnel, or practices of the intelligence system will make the nation proof against surprise attack. The other parts of the overall system of protection are border control both physical and documentary, simple policing, deterrence (which requires identifying something that the enemy values highly and finding ways to destroy it in retaliation for an attack), target hardening and other passive defense measures (including stocking vaccines against lethal pathogens), diplomacy, and rapid-reaction capabilities—"first responders," building evacuation plans, and so forth.[5] These alternatives may be slighted if we are deluded into thinking that by reorganizing the intelligence system we have eliminated the danger of another surprise attack.

One must not be *too* cynical about organizational solutions to perceived enterprise failures. A reorganization might solve, or at least place on the path to solving, a problem that was not

---

5. See generally Bruce Schneier, *Beyond Fear: Thinking Sensibly about Security in an Uncertain World* (2003).

organizational. It might shake up the accustomed ways of doing things in an organization that had become sclerotic, as organizations often do because "people in organizations are talented at normalizing deviant events, at reconciling outliers to a central tendency, at producing plausible displays, at making do with scraps of information, at translating equivocality into feasible alternatives, and at treating as sufficient whatever information is at hand."[6] A reorganization might facilitate needed personnel changes; jobs can be made to disappear in a reorganization without the agency's having to fire the jobholder for cause. But against these benefits must be weighed the costs of transition—including resistance by employees fearful of being reorganized out of a job—and the lulling danger.

We may be able to get some help in thinking about the costs and benefits of restructuring the intelligence system from the scholarly literature on organizations, a literature that the 9/11 Commission disregarded entirely, at least if one may judge from its report. This literature—really, a collection of overlapping literatures—includes organization theory proper, which is an interdisciplinary field to which sociologists, psychologists, economists, and political scientists contribute;[7] a new subfield

6. Richard L. Daft and Karl E. Weick, "Toward a Model of Organizations as Interpretation Systems," 9 *Academy of Management Review* 284, 294 (1984) (citations omitted).

7. See, for example, *Handbook of Organization Studies* (Stewart R. Clegg, Cynthia Hardy, and Walter R. Nord, eds., 1996); L. Peter Jennergren, "Decentralization in Organizations," in *Handbook of Organizational Design*, vol. 2, p. 39 (Paul C. Nystrom and William H. Starbuck, eds., 1981); Arnoldo C. Hax and Nicolas S. Majluf, "Organizational Design: A Survey and an Approach," 29 *Operations Research* 417 (1981); Jacob Marschak and Roy Radner, *Economic Theory of Teams* (1972); Graham T. Allison, *Essence of Decision: Explaining the Cuban Missile Crisis*, ch. 3 (1971). With specific reference to the 9/11 attacks, see Rick Valelly, "How Political Scientists Can Help Fight the War on Terrorism," *Chronicle of Higher Education*, July 19, 2002, p. B10.

of economics called organization economics;[8] the study of
bureaucracy, and of public administration generally, by economists and political scientists, as well as sociologists;[9] a distinct
but related economic literature on motivating employees;[10] and
even a subliterature of organization theory that deals with the
reorganization of government agencies.[11]

Granted, these literatures are rather disappointing, despite
the distinction of many of the contributors. There is heavy reli-

8. See, for example, Luis Garicano, "Hierarchies and the Organization of
Knowledge in Production," 108 *Journal of Political Economy* 874 (2000); Phi-
lippe Aghion and Jean Tirole, "Formal and Real Authority in Organizations,"
105 *Journal of Political Economy* 1 (1997); Jean Tirole, "Hierarchies and
Bureaucracies: On the Role of Collusion in Organizations," 2 *Journal of Law,
Economics, and Organization* 181 (1986).

9. James Q. Wilson, *Bureaucracy: What Government Agencies Do and Why
They Do It* (1989); William A. Niskanen, Jr., *Bureaucracy and Representative
Government* (1971); Anthony Downs, *Inside Bureaucracy* (1967); Gordon Tul-
lock, *The Politics of Bureaucracy* (1965); Jean Tirole, "The Internal Organiza-
tion of Government," 46 *Oxford Economic Papers* (new series) 1 (1994); Raaj
K. Sah, "Fallibility in Human Organizations and Political Systems," *Journal of
Economic Perspectives*, spring 1991, p. 67.

10. See, for example, Beth J. Asch and John T. Warner, "A Theory of Com-
pensation and Personnel Policy in Hierarchical Organizations with Application
to the United States Military," 19 *Journal of Labor Economics* 523 (2001); Jean-
Jacques Laffont and David Martimort, "Collusion and Delegation," 29 *RAND
Journal of Economics* 280 (1998); Canice Prendergast and Robert H. Topel,
"Favoritism in Organizations," 104 *Journal of Political Economy* 958 (1996);
Joseph E. Stiglitz, "Incentives, Information, and Organizational Design," 16
Empirica 3 (1989); George P. Baker, Michael C. Jensen, and Kevin J. Murphy,
"Compensation and Incentives: Practice vs. Theory," 43 *Journal of Finance* 593
(1988).

11. Craig W. Thomas, "Reorganizing Public Organizations: Alternatives,
Objectives, and Evidence," 3 *Journal of Public Administration Research and
Theory* 457 (1993); Ronald C. Moe, *Administrative Renewal: Reorganization
Commissions in the 20th Century* (2003); James Q. Wilson, "Thinking about
Reorganization," in *U.S. Intelligence at the Crossroads: Agendas for Reform* 28
(Roy Godson, Ernest R. May, and Gary Schmitt, eds., 1995); March and Olson,
note 1 above; Steven Maynard-Moody, Donald D. Stull, and Jerry Mitchell,
"Reorganization as Status Drama: Building, Maintaining, and Displacing Dom-
inant Subcultures," 46 *Public Administration Review* 301 (1986).

ance on the case study to the exclusion of more systematic methods of empirical inquiry, and the scholarship tends to be theoretically modest, even platitudinous. (The economic literature on incentives is an exception.) The overarching lesson that emerges from these scholarly literatures is, however, a valuable one: the problems that beset organizations—problems of coordination, control, incentives, the sharing of information, and intelligent decision making—are inherent in conducting activities through organizations and only rarely can they be solved, or even substantially mitigated, by a reorganization.

The purpose of an organization is to coordinate activity, and it is natural to think that an organization is a more efficient method of coordination than leaving things to private ordering—markets, tacit agreements, bargaining, give-and-take, social networks, customs, and the like. Surely, it seems, a central planner could coordinate economic activity better than the market can do, with its business cycles, unemployment, and other symptoms of disequilibrium. But as Friedrich Hayek famously argued and the collapse of communism confirmed, this commonsensical idea is fallacious.[12] The reason is familiar to modern economists (but there were no economists on the 9/11 Commission): knowledge is costly to transfer,[13] especially knowledge that is based on intuition or, what is closely related, involves knowing how to do something rather than knowing facts or procedures that can be communicated as a set of directions. Because of the cost, the manager of a complex system is

12. F. A. Hayek, "The Use of Knowledge in Society," 35 *American Economic Review* 519 (1945).

13. For excellent discussions, see Eric von Hippel, "'Sticky Information' and the Locale of Problem Solving: Implications for Innovation," in *The Dynamic Firm: The Role of Technology, Strategy, Organization, and Regions* 60 (Alfred D. Chandler, Jr., Peter Hagström, and Örjan Sölvell, eds., 1998); Michael C. Jensen and William H. Meckling, "Specific and General Knowledge, and Organizational Structure," *Journal of Applied Finance*, summer 1995, pp. 4, 6–8.

unlikely to have all the information he needs in order to be able to exercise control intelligently.

Hence the importance of decentralized methods of coordination, such as the economic market. New York City is daily supplied with its residents' demand for soap through a network of individual contracts without any individual or firm or government agency controlling the supply of soap and directing its allocation among households. All the dispersed knowledge in this market—each individual consumer's knowledge of his needs and opportunities, each individual seller's knowledge of his costs, his suppliers, his customers—is aggregated by the price system. Suppose a seller, discovering that a particular input needed for the manufacture or distribution of his soap is likely to become scarce, buys up a large quantity of the input and stores it. His action forces up the price of the input, and the higher price induces other users to economize on its use and by thus affecting their costs leads them to raise the price they charge for soap, thereby in effect communicating the information about higher input costs to the entire market. Price operates as a method by which private information is diffused throughout a market and ultimately throughout the entire national and world economy.

Economic markets are the standard example of the effective coordination of complex systems without a coordinator, but not the only one. Language is a system of immense complexity, again with no controller. (Dictionaries and grammars record, often with a lag, parts of the network; they do not create it.) Likewise the Internet, the rules of etiquette, customs, the law (much of which is produced by tacit coordination of judicial decisions), federalism, the international monetary system, the balance of power, cartels, traffic patterns, moral norms.

This is not to deny the importance of business firms and other formal organizations, including government agencies.

Every manufacturer and distributor in New York's soap-supply network, as distinct from the network, or market, itself, is a firm in which hierarchy takes the place of the market as the means of organizing productive activity. Supervisors direct the work of subordinate employees rather than buying their output as in a market system. The pervasiveness of firms and other organizations in a modern economy is compelling evidence that direct control is often a more efficient method of coordinating activity than the market or other decentralized methods.

But only within limits, which is the basic reason why there isn't just one giant business firm, but instead a multitude of firms coordinated not by a central-planning czar but by the invisible hand of the market. Because the span of supervision by one person is limited, the more employees a firm has, the more supervisors it requires; and the more supervisors it has, the more supervisors of supervisors it needs because only so many supervisors can be supervised by one person. So as an organization expands, the layers of supervision multiply. The unavoidable by-products of the lengthening hierarchy of an expanding organization include delay in executing orders, loss of information, attenuation of the directions emanating from the top, and in short a weakening of control and coherence. The larger the organization, moreover, the more difficult it will be to correlate the work of a particular employee with the value of the organization's output, and so the employee's incentives will tend to fall out of alignment with those of the firm. Employees will have scope to engage in behavior that serves their own interests but not those of the firm. This is the problem of agency costs to which I alluded in the last chapter.

The difficulties of controlling an organization are compounded when, as in the case of an intelligence service, the organization's output, not being sold in a market, is difficult to value. Not that market valuations are the only ones on which rational decisions can be based. But whereas the loss of a battle yields valuable information about the army's performance, the information about performance that a failure of intelligence yields is equivocal. We know that even the best intelligence service is bound to be surprised from time to time because the only way to ensure against ever being surprised is to ignore the costs of false alarms and as a result bombard action-level officials with dire warnings. This does not mean that preventive services can never be evaluated. But there is a big difference between competitive suppliers dealing with frequent threats, such as burglar alarm services, so that there is information on which to base an objective comparison of performance, and a monopoly supplier dealing with infrequent threats, which is an approximate description of a nation's intelligence apparatus faced with intermittent threats of attack. In the latter case, comparative performance evaluations will rarely be possible.

The difficulty of valuing an intelligence service's output translates into difficulty in valuing the performance of individual intelligence officers. Baseball is a repetitive activity played under more or less uniform conditions, enabling comparative evaluations of performance. Intelligence is not. The difficulty of evaluating an intelligence officer's performance retards efforts to prevent self-interested behavior that harms the enterprise, behavior such as warping intelligence estimates to conform to superiors' preconceptions, making overly vague predictions, and, relatedly, shying away from issuing warnings—or overwarning in panic situations following a surprise attack. Think of what a joke the color-coded warnings issued by the Department of Homeland Security rapidly became. Too many warnings can, paradoxically, make people feel too safe.

These pathologies are compounded by the difficulty of recruiting superior people to work in intelligence.[14] Intelli-

14. Commission on the Roles and Capabilities of the United States Intelli-

gence is a controversial, indeed a widely unpopular, career in a democratic society. (It doesn't help that government service in general has less appeal to able Americans than to their counterparts in most other societies.) The emphasis on secrecy, on leading a double life, turns off most people. The job pressures are extreme, there is no tenure protection, and melding a career in intelligence with a normal family life is extremely difficult. Promotion opportunities are somewhat truncated because the top layers of government are occupied by political appointees rather than by career civil servants, although many DCIs have been intelligence professionals and below the DCI level there are relatively few political appointees or other lateral entries.

The salary ladder is compressed, which makes it difficult to reward intelligence officers for taking risks, as by making bold predictions. The ladder is compressed by democratic political resistance to compensating government employees generously. Another reason one might expect it to be compressed is that, as in the military, promotions to senior positions (below the political level) in intelligence services are made from within the service rather than by lateral hiring. Salaries must therefore be set high enough to attract people able enough to eventually fill the senior slots. It might seem that because those individuals cannot be identified at the outset, all beginning employees would be "overpaid,"[15] making it difficult, given budget constraints, to pay appropriately high salaries to the senior employees. In fact, however, entry-level salaries in intelligence services are modest, suggesting that nonpecuniary income is a major element of the total income of an intelligence officer. (A further indication is that despite the modest

gence Community, *Preparing for the 21st Century: An Appraisal of U.S. Intelligence* 87 (Mar. 1, 1996), at www.access.gpo.gov/int/pdf/.

15. Asch and Warner, note 10 above, at 551.

salaries, the CIA, for example, has almost 10 times as many job applicants as it has jobs to fill.) But this may increase the fragility of intelligence officers' morale; the monetary salary may not be high enough to compensate for a loss of nonpecuniary income as a result of public criticisms, frequent shakeups in the managerial ranks, increased job pressures, or other adverse changes in the work environment.

The loss of control over a workforce as hierarchy lengthens tends to create a diseconomy of scale,[16] hierarchy and size marching in lockstep because of the limitation on the span of control that I noted earlier. But there is an alternative to hierarchy that is important in the intelligence field because the potential agency costs are high and also because, as I'll explain later, intelligence requires qualities of originality and imagination that do not flourish in hierarchical, bureaucratized organizations. That alternative is to decentralize the organization, in imitation of the market, as by delegating authority to division heads and requiring them to compete with one another for allocations of capital from central management, or from Congress in the case of a federal agency.

The next step in decentralization is to make the autonomous divisions separate agencies, a process visible in the history of the intelligence services of the United States and other countries. The more heterogeneous the activities of different divisions in an agency, the more likely they are to evolve into freestanding agencies. The design and launching of spy satellites, for example, require such different skills, procedures, and facilities from those required for intelligence analysis that combining the two functions, each essential to intelligence, in one

16. See, for a good discussion, Oliver E. Williamson, "Hierarchical Control and Optimum Firm Size," 75 *Journal of Political Economy* 123 (1967).

agency (let alone one division) would yield no economies of scale or scope.[17] It would merely exacerbate the diseconomies associated with very large, heterogeneous organizations. The tendency of public agencies to fission, and thus of the number of agencies to increase, as government grows is efficient because of the diseconomies of large scale. This point is overlooked in proposals, by no means limited to the intelligence area, to consolidate government functions in fewer, but larger, agencies.

In the economic and business literature the issue of optimal centralization is often posed as a choice between the "U-form" ("U" for unitary) and the "M-form" ("M" for multidivisional) of organization. In the first, functional divisions, such as research, production, and sales, are coordinated at the top of the organization. In the second, each division operates as a more or less self-contained producer, such as the Chevrolet and Buick divisions of General Motors;[18] top management does not coordinate functions directly but maintains control by monitoring the costs, revenues, and profits of each division and intervening in a division's operations when those indicators reveal inadequate performance.[19] The U-form is less nimble because infor-

---

17. Economies of scale are present when increasing the size of an entity reduces its average costs, economies of scope when increasing the number of different products or services produced by the company reduces its average costs.

18. Alfred P. Sloan, Jr., *My Years with General Motors* (1963).

19. The classic of this literature is Alfred D. Chandler, Jr., *Strategy and Structure: Chapters in the History of the American Industrial Enterprise* (1962); for reconsideration, see Robert F. Freeland, "The Myth of the M-Form? Governance, Consent, and Organizational Change," 102 *American Journal of Sociology* 483 (1996). Economic analysis of the U-form/M-form distinction was pioneered by Oliver Williamson. See, for example, Oliver E. Williamson, *Corporate Control and Business Behavior: An Inquiry into the Effects of Organization Form on Enterprise Behavior* (1970); Oliver E. Williamson, *Markets and Hierarchies: Analysis and Antitrust Implications* (1975).

mation must travel up the hierarchy from the different functional divisions to be integrated at the top and, after being converted there into directives, must travel back down again to the divisions for implementation. The U-form is preferable for routinized activities that can be supervised by a handful of highly competent executives, the M-form for activities that require a high level of competence and initiative at the operating level as well. A pertinent risk created by the U-form, as by dictatorship, is that of deferring excessively to the judgment of a single person—the lesson of the failure of Israeli intelligence to anticipate the 1973 surprise attack[20]—and in the case of the Director of National Intelligence, the judgment of an overworked person.

The intelligence system cannot be organized in the pure M-form, as a collection of intelligence services equivalent to the automotive-brand divisions of General Motors, if only because some of the services stand in the relation of supplier or customer to one another rather than producing similar outputs. The National Reconnaissance Office, which designs, builds, and launches spy satellites, produces a very different output from the CIA. But some of the intelligence agencies produce similar, indeed competitive, outputs. For example, the CIA, the Defense Intelligence Agency, the National Intelligence Council, and the State Department's Bureau of Intelligence and Research are all engaged in what has accurately been termed "competitive analysis."[21] To that extent the intelligence system is organized in the M-form. The creation of another layer of hierarchy would, by strengthening authority at the top, reduce

20. Uri Bar-Joseph, "Intelligence Failure and the Need for Cognitive Closure: The Case of Yom Kippur," in *Paradoxes of Strategic Intelligence: Essays in Honor of Michael I. Handel* 166 (Richard K. Betts and Thomas G. Mahnken, eds., 2003).

21. Mark M. Lowenthal, *Intelligence: From Secrets to Policy* 13, 89 (2000).

initiative and speed of response at the bottom. If the paean to unification in the 9/11 Commission's report, the hortatory provisions of the President's August 2004 executive orders, the Intelligence Reform Act itself, and the President's remarks at the signing ceremony[22] are all taken seriously, the thrust of the post-9/11 "reforms" has been to move the intelligence system toward the U-form.

A particular danger caused by adding layers to an intelligence system comes from the boy-crying-wolf phenomenon that I keep harping on. In every organization, information is filtered as it rises in the organization's hierarchy[23]—the top would be flooded if it received all the information generated at the lowest level. The more layers there are, the less information that will reach the top, where the decisions are made. Given the normal reluctance of intelligence officers to issue warnings of a surprise attack, the insertion of an additional layer—the Director of National Intelligence and his large staff—in the intelligence hierarchy is likely to cause a further dilution of warning signals. This will impair the ability of the policymakers to take timely action to prevent attacks, though as long as the intelligence services continue on hyperalert for another 9/11, this danger may not be great.

The additional layer will also, however, increase the distance between the producers and the consumers of intelligence, causing potentially dangerous delays even if there is no filtering (but there will be also an increased risk of misunderstandings), and thus retarding the process by which raw intelligence data become processed into coherent, "actionable" information for policymakers.

22. "President Signs Intelligence Reform and Terrorism Prevention Act," Dec. 17, 2004, at www.whitehouse.gov/news/releases/2004/12/20041217-1.html.

23. Kenneth J. Arrow, *The Limits of Organization* 53–54 (1974).

That is not the only kind of delay that the additional layer of supervision will add. The tactics used by the CIA's Directorate of Operations, the clandestine branch of the agency, are at times dangerous, politically sensitive (for example, they may involve "snatching" a person off the street of a foreign country, breaking into an embassy, or firing a missile from a Predator at a suspected terrorist), and time-sensitive. Intelligence officers may have to call the CIA's director for immediate permission to act. Will he feel obliged, as a matter of prudence, to consult the DNI? As a practical matter, then, will two permission slips be required? If so, the additional delay could spoil important missions.

The additional supervisory layer will also exacerbate the tendency of local commanders—vital consumers of intelligence, for they may be the only officials in a position to thwart an attack—to ignore warnings from Washington. The greater the distance (cultural, organizational) between center and periphery, the likelier the consumers of intelligence are to dismiss the analyst's assessment on the ground that he is too remote to be knowledgeable about local conditions or that he's pursuing his own agenda.[24]

I don't mean to slight the importance of coordination, not only between agencies that stand in a supply relationship to one another, but also—because of the need for pooling fragmentary data in order to make accurate threat assessments— between parallel, "competitive" agencies. Achieving coordination is difficult because the agencies view their relation-

---

24. Bruce D. Berkowitz and Allan E. Goodman, *Strategic Intelligence for American National Security* 59–63 (1989). "Centralization [of intelligence] violates what to me is the single most important principle of successful intelligence, i.e. closeness of intelligence producers to intelligence users or consumers." Sherman Kent, *Strategic Intelligence for American World Policy* 81 (1949).

ship as primarily one of competing for limited budgetary resources. In a competitive market, a firm grows and thrives by satisfying consumer demands better than its competitors do. But a government agency grows and thrives by persuading politicians to increase its budget.[25] A bureaucrat who does not advocate forcefully for his agency risks stagnation or decline in the agency's budget, and even if his salary and job security are not affected, his career satisfaction, which is a major form of remuneration for ambitious bureaucrats, will suffer grievously.

Hence the phenomenon of the turf war.[26] Competition between government agencies tends to be more bitter than competition between firms because it is competition in advocacy rather than in selling better products at lower prices. If your competitor is selling a better product, passionate advocacy of your product, politicking, indignant denunciation of the competitor, and a blind commitment to your way of doing business will not bring you success. But if you are a bureaucrat, such behavior may win you a turf war. Not that turf wars are altogether a bad thing. One way to prevail is to convince by honest argument and truthful evidence whatever higher authority carves up turf that your agency should be given the additional responsibility that it seeks.[27] Were it not for turf wars the 9/11 Commission's organizational recommendations would have been enacted into law even sooner than they were and with fewer modifications. But often turf warriors decide they're better off colluding than competing, presenting the higher authority not with a choice but with the bureaucratic equivalent of a

25. A major theme of Niskanen, note 9 above.

26. The literature on turf wars is surprisingly limited, given their frequency and importance. For rare illustrations, see David C. King, *Turf Wars: How Congressional Committees Claim Jurisdiction* (1997); Harvey Robbins, *Turf Wars: Moving from Competition to Collaboration* (1992).

27. On the advantages of competitive over monopolistic bureaucracy, see Niskanen, note 9 above, at 197–201, 228.

division of markets. That may explain the remarkable fact that although military technology and threats keep changing, the shares of the U.S. defense budget of the three major uniformed services are approximately the same year after year.[28]

Turf wars in government resemble turf wars between street gangs. In both cases the competitors cannot rely on the usual market- and law-based methods, such as the creation and enforcement of property and contract rights, of obtaining resources, so they are forced to turn to alternatives that cost more.[29] The costs take different forms. But just as the arrest of a gang's leaders may precipitate a turf war, with competing gangs fighting to take advantage of the opportunities created by the weakening of the gang, so the reorganization of a government agency may, by shifting boundaries between subunits, incite a protracted struggle over how to redraw the boundaries. It is appalling, but to a student of government reorganization unsurprising, that it took two years for the FBI and the New York City police and health departments to agree on an allocation of responsibilities for investigating suspected biological attacks.[30]

I have emphasized size and heterogeneity as limits on the optimal degree of centralization. In addition, diseconomies of scope are encountered when inconsistent missions are combined in a single organization—intelligence and counterintelligence, for example. An intelligence officer uses spies or other

28. Center for Strategic Budgetary Assessments, "DoD Budget by Service, FY 1980–2003" (Feb. 2002), at www.csbaonline.org/3Defense Budget/2Tables Graphs/5Service Budgets/Graph2.pdf.

29. Steven D. Levitt and Sudhir Alladi Venkatesh, "An Economic Analysis of a Drug-Selling Gang's Finances," 115 *Quarterly Journal of Economics* 755, 780–781 (2000).

30. Judith Miller, "City and F.B.I. Reach Agreement on Bioterror Investigations," *New York Times* (late ed.), Nov. 21, 2004, p. 39.

means of penetration or surveillance to obtain what he hopes is truthful information about a potential threat, while the counterintelligence officer tries to show that the spy is a double agent whose information is disinformation. The counterintelligence officer is, in an expressive bit of unofficial bureaucratic lingo, the "office asshole."[31] Another example of mission incompatibility within the same agency is the placement of both criminal investigations and domestic intelligence in the FBI, discussed in the next chapter.

"Incompatibility" in this context need not imply animosity or even rivalry. It need only imply missions so different that placing them in the same agency may cause them to be performed badly simply because of the organizational imperative of minimum uniformity. An organization is apt to be ungovernable if its employees do their jobs in completely different ways, governed by different systems of compensation, promotion, supervision, etc. No large organization can be held together except by rules that impose a degree of uniformity on its personnel; if the rules are to govern without causing unbearable strain, the personnel must have some underlying homogeneity of skills, attitudes, tasks, ambitions, habits, and character. That is why the same companies don't produce software and hubcaps, locomotives and cat food, pharmaceutical drugs and elementary education.

There is mission incompatibility even in combining intelligence collection and intelligence analysis, and even though the analyst needs more than the raw data—he needs to know where they came from so that he can determine their reliability—while the collector needs the analyst to tell him what to

31. On the lowly status of counterintelligence in intelligence agencies, see Gregory F. Treverton, *Reshaping National Intelligence for an Age of Information* 146 (2001); Roy Godson, "Intelligence: An American View," in *British and American Approaches to Intelligence* 3, 13 (K. G. Robertson, ed., 1987).

collect. The collector will be reluctant to disclose his sources to the analyst because disclosure might reveal a spy's identity, jeopardizing his life should the identification leak, or reveal that an enemy's code has been broken, which if discovered by the enemy would lead him to change the code. Moreover, the type of person who operates undercover, runs spies, organizes coups, and engages in or manages other risky clandestine activities is likely to have a different psychology from a desk-bound intelligence analyst; he is the man of action versus the man of thought, the warrior versus the intellectual. The difference is likely to breed distrust and misunderstanding, impeding communication and cooperation. Code breakers and other technicians likewise have little in common with clandestine operators, who are likely moreover to dominate the agency (that has been the experience with the CIA)[32]—and not simply because they are more aggressive. They are likely to be abler. People with a high level of analytic skills can find all sorts of attractive jobs in the private sector, making it difficult for an intelligence service to compete. People with a proclivity for clandestine operations—and there are some very able people with that unusual taste—can find good jobs in the private sector too (in part because of the demand by defense contractors for employees who are cleared to handle classified materials), but they cannot easily find jobs that yield the same nonpecuniary income that they derive from their intelligence career.

These tensions might seem to argue for breaking up the CIA not merely into three pieces, as recommended by Senator

32. Peter Szanton et al., "Intelligence: Seizing the Opportunity," 22 *Foreign Policy* 183, 195–196 (1976). In addition, "operators have more influence in decision making but are less capable of unbiased interpretation of evidence because they have a vested interest in the success of their operation; autonomous analysts are more disinterested and usually more objective, but lack influence." Richard K. Betts, "Analysis, War, and Decision: Why Intelligence Failures Are Inevitable," 31 *World Politics* 61, 67 (1978).

Roberts, but into four (operations, analysis, technical, and counterintelligence) or even five (if the Special Activities Division, the paramilitary branch of the CIA, were shifted to the Defense Department, as the 9/11 Commission recommended, though its recommendation didn't make it into the Intelligence Reform Act). But that would be a mistake, and not only because the more intelligence agencies there are, the more difficult coordination and control become. (There can be too few agencies because of diseconomies of scale, but there can also be too many because of the limits of control—we can begin to sense the difficulty of designing, let alone implementing, worthwhile organizational reforms.) The relationship between collectors and analysts of intelligence, fraught as it is, is too intimate to justify sundering them into different agencies. This is especially so because the analysts are also collectors. They integrate separate pieces of data received from the collectors and thus generate more data, and they also obtain additional data directly, from open-source materials. I emphasized the dependence of analysis on the reliability of sources; if analysts and collectors are in separate agencies, the collectors will be even more reluctant than they are now to disclose their sources to the analysts. Rivalrous though they are, the analysts and collectors in the CIA have more sense of a common purpose than they would have were they in separate agencies.

The barriers to information sharing would also be greater. Those barriers are an aspect of the more general problem of information transfer that I discussed with reference to Hayek's critique of central planning—the sheer epistemic difficulty of communicating one's knowledge, much of which may be tacit and so below the possessor's threshold of conscious awareness. Placing the transferors and transferees of intelligence data in different agencies would increase the inherent difficulty of transferring knowledge. This is a compelling argument for retaining the technical and paramilitary personnel of the CIA in that agency, as well as the analysts, especially given how hazy the line is that separates clandestine collection of intelligence from clandestine actions based on intelligence information. It will be unfortunate if the Director of National Intelligence uses his generous staff allotment to divert the cream of the CIA's analytic work into his own shop.

Coordination of intelligence agencies is an imperative; centralization may not be. Before the Intelligence Reform Act, the agencies were coordinated in a variety of ways (most of which will continue): through committees in the executive branch, such as the National Security Council and, though much less important, the President's Foreign Intelligence Advisory Board and Intelligence Oversight Board; through the Office of Management and Budget, which coordinates the budget proposals of the different departments and agencies in the executive branch; through a variety of ad hoc task forces and informal contacts; through congressional committees; by the CIA director in his capacity as Director of Central Intelligence and thus the chairman of the board of the intelligence community; within the CIA through fusion centers, such as the Counterintelligence Center; and through fusion centers outside the CIA, such as the National Intelligence Council and the new National Counterterrorism Center, which supersedes the CIA's Terrorist Threat Integration Center.[33] So loose a system of coordination was bound to produce gaps and overlaps, but the latter, at least, are not necessarily a bad thing to have.[34] Redundancy is a stan-

33. See generally Federation of American Scientists, "US Intelligence and Security Agencies" (June 4, 2004), at www.fas.org/irp/official.html. Remember that the NCTC was created by President Bush before its creation was reordained by the Intelligence Reform Act.

34. Martin Landau, "Redundancy, Rationality, and the Problem of Duplica-

dard method of increasing safety, and safety is the business of intelligence.

Tighter coordination may well be desirable in one phase of the intelligence process, however. I mentioned in Chapter 2 the surprising suggestion in a recent newspaper article that the real significance of the creation of a Director of National Intelligence is that it may enable better integration of the different *technical* means of intelligence. The point was not emphasized by the 9/11 Commission but is a useful reminder of the importance of coordination at the collection stage of the intelligence process. What is euphemistically termed "human intelligence" (i.e., spies) is, of course, simply one method among many for collecting intelligence data; spy satellites and other listening and seeing devices (such as electronic eavesdropping equipment on naval vessels and other platforms, and cameras in high-flying aircraft), collecting both image data and signal data, are another; military attachés (the province of the Defense Intelligence Agency) a third; reading technical journals a fourth; and so on. None of these sources has priority, and the data obtained by them must be pooled for reliable inferences to be drawn. The problem of coordination posed by the multiplicity of sources has less to do with pooling the data collected from the different sources than with coordinating the collection systems themselves, which, apart from the spies and attachés and readers of open-source materials, are complex, costly, R&D-intensive, and require long lead times to build and deploy yet are scattered among different agencies. For exam-

---

tion and Overlap," 29 *Public Administration Review* 346 (1969). Of course, the costs can exceed the benefits, as I have argued is the case with overlapping federal and state enforcement of antitrust laws. Richard A. Posner, "Federalism and the Enforcement of Antitrust Laws by State Attorneys General," in *Competition Laws in Conflict: Antitrust Jurisdiction in the Global Economy* 252 (Richard A. Epstein and Michael S. Greve, eds., 2004).

ple, the same photons collected by spy satellites are used by the National Reconnaissance Office to make photographs and by the National Geospatial-Intelligence Agency to make maps. Improving our technical means of intelligence has become urgent because of the technological sophistication of al Qaeda and because monitoring electronic communications is becoming more difficult as a result of increased volume, advances in encryption, and the advent of the cell phone, which has no fixed locus and is easily disposed of after the first call.

The required coordination cannot be performed adequately by a White House official or the director of the CIA. It could have been made a special focus of a Director of Central Intelligence sprung free from having to run the CIA. Another special focus (to recall the brief discussion in Chapter 2) might be on coordinating domestic with foreign intelligence. The DNI will be too busy to focus on either project, however, if he takes a broad view of his powers and in particular if he injects himself into substantive intelligence issues, as he will have to do if he wants to give competent briefings to the President rather than allow that task to continue to be performed by the director of the CIA.

This last point invites attention to a drawback to centralizing intelligence that is especially serious given the sheer size of the U.S. intelligence system: overloading the top of the intelligence hierarchy. The Director of National Intelligence will have his hands more than full if besides supervising the nation's vast and heterogeneous intelligence apparatus—which will mean umpiring endless turf wars, as well as fighting his own turf wars with such powerful rivals as the Secretary of Defense—he must brief the President weekly or daily on the latest intelligence, as well as testify before the congressional committees (numerous—and unlikely to surrender any of their turf!) concerned with intelligence matters.

Let us pause for a moment on the matter of briefing the President. Quite apart from other calls on his time, the DNI will be too remote from the operating level of the intelligence system to be able to give the President more than a thirdhand briefing unless he immerses himself in substantive matters to the degree that most DCIs, such as George Tenet, have done. But he will be reluctant to relinquish the briefing responsibility to the director of the CIA, for then that official will establish a closer relationship with the President than the DNI, reducing the latter's effective authority. This problem would not arise if all Congress had done was to authorize the President to separate the post of Director of Central Intelligence from that of CIA director, for the "liberated" DCI would have been a board chairman, whereas the DNI is likely to view himself as more like a CEO, which will make him a rival of a CIA director, who *is* the CEO of the intelligence agency that will continue to regard itself as central and fight to retain (or regain) that position.

Most of the DNI's time may be spent patrolling the tense border between his domain and the Defense Department. The principal intelligence agencies other than the CIA reside in the department. Their budgets are components of the department's overall budget. The 9/11 Commission wanted the Director of National Intelligence to control the budgets of those agencies except insofar as the agencies are concerned with merely tactical military intelligence. But the line between tactical and strategic military intelligence is indistinct.[35] What I am calling "tactical intelligence," and what the Intelligence Reform Act, following the line drawn by the 9/11 Commission's report, excludes from the DNI's budgetary authority, consists of two

35. On the complex structure of defense intelligence, see Walter Jajko, "The Future of Defense Intelligence," in *U.S. Intelligence at the Crossroads: Agendas for Reform* 214 (Roy Godson, Ernest R. May, and Gary Schmitt, eds., 1995).

conglomerations of programs: the Tactical Intelligence and Related Activities Program (TIARA) and the Joint Military Intelligence Program (JMIP).[36] The former consists of the intelligence programs of the various uniformed services dedicated to the support of tactical operations. The latter consists of a variety of cryptographic, photographic, and mapping programs designed to support multiservice or defense-wide operations, and it is unclear in what sense those programs should be regarded as tactical rather than strategic. However classified, they overlap the intelligence programs that the DNI would like to control because they yield information that bears on terrorist and other threats to the nation as well as information relating to specific military operations as in Iraq or Afghanistan.

The 9/11 Commission's proposal that subordinates of cabinet officers be appointed to two of the DNI's three deputy directorships was intended in part to minimize conflict with the Defense Department, for one of the deputies was to be the Undersecretary of Defense for Intelligence. But the proposal would if adopted have nudged the intelligence system toward what organization theorists call a "matrix" system of control—and point out is fraught with difficulties.[37] The dual-hatting proposals were rejected by Congress, probably correctly; but the uneasy relationship of the DNI to the Defense Department remains a bulit-in feature of the reorganized system.

The 9/11 Commission blamed the failure to anticipate the 9/11 attacks mainly on inadequate sharing of intelligence among the different intelligence agencies and thought a more centralized

36. For a good description of these programs, see GlobalSecurity.org., "Intelligence Budget," at www/globalsecurity.org/intell/library/budget/ (visited Jan. 6, 2005).

37. Arnoldo C. Hax and Nicolas S. Majluf, "Organizational Design: A Survey and an Approach," 29 *Operations Research* 417, 428–431 (1981).

intelligence structure an indispensable part of the cure. The cure may not fit the disease. The different intelligence agencies are not actually being merged, and anyway information sometimes flows more freely between organizations than within them. The problem of sharing intelligence information is almost as acute within agencies like the CIA (recall the reluctance of the operations branch to share information with the analytic branch), and especially the FBI, as between agencies— and in the case of the FBI, maybe more so. An agency's sense of common mission can be occluded by internal tensions. The criminal investigators in the FBI may feel more threatened by the Bureau's intelligence officers than by the Border Patrol in the Department of Homeland Security and may be more willing to cooperate with local police, who are engaged in the same kind of work as they, than with the Bureau's own intelligence officers. Competition for budget may be more intense within than across agencies, and likewise jockeying for the attention and support of superiors.

Any benefits in the way of better sharing of intelligence among intelligence agencies as a result of greater centralization are likely, moreover, to be purchased at the cost of increased uniformity in personnel policies, intelligence methods, and organizational traditions and cultures. Those cultures can differ markedly; the State Department, the culture of which could not be more different from that of the CIA, has its own intelligence agency, the Bureau of Intelligence and Research. Although I am calling uniformity a "cost," it might seem a very good thing simply on grounds of economy. But differences among agencies in practices, recruitment, traditions, and other characteristics that give an organization a unique perspective promote not only competitive energy and team spirit but also diversity of approach, perspective, and outlook. Maybe diverse agencies don't share information as well as agencies do that are as like one another as peas in a pod (though this is uncertain), but maybe they produce more and better information, and the benefit may exceed the cost.

How might diversity promote the production of information? Consider innovation in the private sector, now widely understood as a quasi-Darwinian process: one almost of trial and error, in which the market selects from among diverse approaches whose relative promise cannot be assessed in advance,[38] much as nature selects from among variant competing life-forms—the products of random mutation—those best adapted to their environment. The greater the diversity of life-forms to choose from, the more rapid and complete the adaptation to the environment, corresponding in human society to maximizing welfare through technological progress. Completing the analogy, a multiplicity of independent sources of inventive activity may be superior to a centralized process. Consider "high-flex" Silicon Valley firms, with their "change culture upon which there is great consensus. They will have shallow hierarchies and significant local autonomy. Such firms will resist the hierarchical accouterments of seniority and rank—and they will resist functional specialization which restricts the flow of ideas and destroys the sense of commonality of purpose."[39]

Another word for innovation is information, which is a synonym for intelligence—so the business of an intelligence system is innovation; and the system is likely to be more productive to the extent that it consists of diverse and not

38. See, for example, Richard R. Nelson and Sidney G. Winter, *An Evolutionary Theory of Economic Change* (1982); Nelson and Winter, "Evolutionary Theorizing in Economics," *Journal of Economic Perspectives*, spring 2002, pp. 23, 33–39.

39. David J. Teece, "Design Issues for Innovative Firms: Bureaucracy, Incentives and Industrial Structure," in *The Dynamic Firm*, note 13 above, at 134, 154.

merely multiple producers. Remember that perception is a selection, from the mass of sense data, that is guided by preconception. A diversity of preconceptions will generate a richer selection of relevant information to analyze and a broader range of perspectives among the analysts. We want analysts to be sampling from the broadest possible range of data and to be drawing inferences from their samples with different mindsets. Differently acculturated intelligence officers will notice different things. So here is a potential benefit of limiting sharing of information among intelligence officers: to avoid premature consensus. It is also an argument for encouraging some mid-career lateral entry into the CIA.

Another name for preconception, one that ties intelligence more directly to innovation, is theory. We make sense of the world by formulating theories to explain and predict phenomena. The theories are influenced by facts, but once formulated they become lenses through which to view and interpret new facts. If the theories are wrong, the interpretations they impose will impede the process by which theories are overthrown by confrontation with inconvenient facts. Whether the theory is that the Japanese threat to Pearl Harbor is sabotage or that al Qaeda will only attack the U.S. overseas, the falsity of the theory is the critical obstacle to anticipating the attack, because the theory obscures, dissolves, and distorts facts that would otherwise raise a warning flag. So we want an intelligence culture in which the regnant theories are constantly being challenged, not by devil's advocates, who are merely stage challengers, but by people who really see the world differently; and for those people to have a voice and be heard—for a genuine clash of theories to occur, as in science—requires a diverse intelligence system, implying a flat structure with loose rather than tight control over its component parts.

Diversity is difficult to achieve within a single agency

because, as I pointed out earlier, effective control of an organization requires imposing a high degree of uniformity on the
employees. Large organizations are bureaucracies governed by
rules that can furnish clear guidance only by abstracting from
many of the different ways in which particular tasks might be
performed and particular employees compensated, motivated,
supervised, and so on, and establishing uniform pay scales,
working conditions, retirement programs, promotion criteria.
The need for uniformity is another way of explaining why heterogeneity limits the expansion of organizations. In principle,
a single organization could be loose knit, permitting a thousand
flowers to bloom within it—more like a confederation, an alliance, than like an organization. But in practice, at least in large
organizations, the centrifugal forces would be too great; some
minimum homogeneity is necessary if management is to maintain control.

The 9/11 Commission did not propose fusing all our intelligence services into a single agency. But the CEO-like role that
it envisaged for the Director of National Intelligence conceived
of the different services as being like the divisions of a single
business firm. How far unification will proceed under the Intelligence Reform Act is, at this writing, unclear. But maybe too
far. For although it isn't possible to model the U.S. intelligence
system on a "high-flex" Silicon Valley firm, the system could
be gravely weakened by being moved too far in the opposite
direction, toward the tight bureaucracy symbolized by the U.S.
Postal Service. The DNI may want to move it in that direction
in order to maximize his control.

To recognize the drawbacks of a centralized system of intelligence might seem to make the case for a decentralized system—for "pluralism," as it is called. The Agranat Commission
as we know recommended that Israel move toward pluralism—

then as now (or at least until the Intelligence Reform Act is fully implemented) the character of the U.S. system. Yet our system, which also monitored the military activities of Egypt and Syria in 1973, and with more resources (if less intensity) than Israel, equally failed to predict the attack[40]—hardly an advertisement for pluralism! One reason a pluralist system may fail despite its advantages over a centralized one is that it presents policymakers with more choices. This can be good, but it also can be bad; by arming the policymakers to allow their own priors to shape decision, it exacerbates the tendency of high officials to make their own, uninformed intelligence estimates, disregarding expert advice. This appears to have been a factor in still another recent intelligence failure—the failure to anticipate the insurgency in Iraq that followed the successful U.S. invasion.

Another thing that blurs the choice between a centralized and a pluralist system of intelligence is that the danger of leaks and moles increases with the size of the organization. The antidote is compartmentalization. But compartmentalization impedes the circulation of information within the organization, thus making its subunits more autonomous—and thus making a large intelligence organization functionally similar to a series of small ones.

The startling implication of this discussion is that the performance of a nation's intelligence system is probably, within a broad range, insensitive to how it is organized. It is not only that centralization and pluralism both have weaknesses and, more important, that history seems not to vindicate one over the other (or any intermediate position, either); it is, more broadly, that *no* known organizational form seems able to cope

40. Richard K. Betts, *Surprise Attack: Lessons for Defense Planning* 288 (1982).

well with problems of information and incentives as grave as those that beset the intelligence function. The literature on government reorganizations[41] describes a litany of failures, though the government functions involved were easier to perform than the intelligence function.

But while centralization and pluralism may thus enjoy a certain abstract parity in the analysis of "ideal" intelligence systems, the particular centralizing moves adopted by Congress in response to the 9/11 Commission's recommendations seem undesirable, quite apart from transition costs, in comparison to more modest centralizing moves, such as augmenting the powers of the Director of Central Intelligence along the lines that I have suggested in this chapter.

The 9/11 Commission's only example of a successful centralizing reorganization was the Goldwater-Nichols Department of Defense Reorganization Act of 1986.[42] That act—which provided the template for the commission's organizational recommendations—strengthened the central control of the armed forces by greatly expanding the power of the Chairman of the Joint Chiefs of Staff vis-à-vis the service chiefs (army chief of staff, etc.). Though the act seems to have been, on balance, a success—even if not the unalloyed one that the commission supposed it to be—it is not an apt model for a reorganization of intelligence. It was passed in response to a series of disasters definitely attributable to a lack of cooperation between the different military services—the failure of the Iranian hostage rescue mission (1980), the bombing of the U.S. Marine barracks in Beirut (1982), and the communications snafus that beset the Grenada operation (1983). These fiascoes were convincing evidence that interservice rivalry had gone too far. Even so,

41. See note 11 above.
42. Comprehensively discussed in Gordon Nathaniel Lederman, *Reorganizing the Joint Chiefs of Staff: The Goldwater-Nichols Act of 1986* (1999).

despite the successes that increased centralization yielded in our two wars with Iraq and the 2001 campaign in Afghanistan, there has been a downside: serious mistakes in our operations in Panama (1989), the first Iraq war (1991), and Somalia (1993) have been attributed to excessive authority wielded by Colin Powell as Chairman of the Joint Chiefs throughout the period covered by these operations.[43]

We know from Chapter 1 that the failure to anticipate the 9/11 attacks was probably not due to the way in which the U.S. intelligence system is organized, unless it is the siting of our domestic security service in the FBI, an organizational anomaly that the 9/11 Commission did not propose to eliminate. The Goldwater-Nichols Act offered a solution to a demonstrated organizational problem; the 9/11 Commission's organizational recommendations seem, rather, to reflect a desperate hope that the nonorganizational problems of our intelligence system can be solved by a reorganization.

Also, the idea for the Goldwater Nichols Act originated within the armed forces themselves[44] (though resisted by Reagan's defense secretary, Caspar Weinberger). The literature on reorganizations teaches that a reorganization is more likely to be successful if it is proposed by the agency that is to be reorganized.[45] Insiders know more, and a reorganization proposed by outsiders and resisted by insiders is likely to be responding

43. Thomas L. McNaugher with Roger L. Sperry, "Improving Military Coordination: The Goldwater-Nichols Reorganization of the Department of Defense," in *Who Makes Policy: The Struggle for Control between Congress and the Executive* 219 (Robert S. Gilmour and Alexis A. Halley, eds., 1994); Frank Hoffman, "Goldwater-Nichols after a Decade," in *The Emerging Strategic Environment: Challenges of the Twenty-First Century* 156 (Williamson Murray, ed., 1999).

44. Lederman, note 42 above, chs. 2–3.

45. Frederick C. Mosher, "Part Two: Analytical Commentary," in *Governmental Reorganizations: Cases and Commentary* 475, 514 (Frederick C. Mosher, ed., 1967).

to imperatives unrelated to efficiency—the felt need, in the 9/11 Commission's case, to propose something dramatic, and in the case of Congress to *do* something dramatic in response to the commission's report.

A related point is that the act was a response to a demand by dissatisfied "consumers" of the "product" of the entity to be reorganized. Its origin was a complaint by Chairman of the Joint Chiefs David Jones that he could not do his job properly within the existing organizational framework. The legislators who pushed first for the creation of the 9/11 Commission and then for the passage of the Intelligence Reform Act were not the consumers of intelligence. The consumers are the officials responsible for the defense of the nation. They did not seek a reorganization of the intelligence system either before or after 9/11.

Nor does the success of the Goldwater-Nichols reorganization prove that greater centralization is an irresistible tide in national security affairs. The breaking off of the Air Force from the Army, which was part of the reorganization that created the Department of Defense in 1947, was a decentralizing move—as was, for that matter, the creation that same year of a freestanding intelligence agency, separate from the military departments and services, namely the CIA. The Goldwater-Nichols Act was, moreover, the culmination of almost 40 years of gradually increasing centralization of the armed forces (beginning with the creation of the Defense Department—and some important centralizing moves, such as the creation of a Chairman of the Joint Chiefs of Staff, had come earlier, during World War II), and it took many years to achieve the act's aim of eliminating lethal interservice rivalries. Furthermore, the armed forces vastly eclipse, in size and budget, the intelligence agencies, and have a very different output. There is no reason to think that the two sectors, though both are concerned with national security, should be organized in similar ways.

Still another reason to question the wisdom of reorganizing the intelligence system is that nominal and real organizational bonds need not coincide. A table of organization may conceal more than it reveals—may conceal all sorts of informal relationships that have evolved in response to changes in circumstances that the designers of the table haven't caught up with.[46] Redoing the table to conform to the new circumstances can clarify channels of communication and command if it is done right, but it may well be done wrong, disrupting relationships that constitute the real organization. The history of reorganizations underscores this danger.

That formal differences in organization may not have much effect on the efficiency of an intelligence system is the lesson of the debate over centralized versus pluralist systems and is one reason the effects of a reorganization tend to be exaggerated in anticipation.

There is nothing to support the optimistic view that the 9/11 Commission's structural recommendations would if adopted have broken the mold or that the modified form in which they were enacted by Congress will do so either. The

46. John S. Brown and Paul Duguid, "Organizational Learning and Communities-of-Practice: Toward a Unified View of Working, Learning, and Innovation," 2 *Organization Science* 40 (1991); Ronald Fraser, "Reorganizing the Organization Chart," 38 *Public Administration Review* 280 (1978). "Organizational sociologists have long emphasized the distinction between formal and informal aspects of organizational structure. Formal aspects include official job descriptions and reporting relationships, as well as formal contracts. Informal aspects include norms and mutual understandings, as well as networks of nonreporting relationships among individuals. Roughly speaking, the formal structure is the organization chart, whereas the informal structure is the way things really work." Robert Gibbons, "Why Organizations Are Such a Mess (and What an Economist Might Do About It)" 35 (Sloan School, Massachusetts Institute of Technology, Mar. 23, 2000).

structural changes made by the Intelligence Reform Act are clumsy and bureaucratizing, may warp or even dissolve in the battles over implementation that are already beginning,[47] and are likely to to generate transition costs far in excess of foreseeable benefits.

47. See, for example, Eric Schmitt, "Pentagon Sends Own Spy Units into Battlefield: Role May Encroach on Territory of CIA," *New York Times* (national ed.), Jan. 24, 2005, p. A1; Barton Gellman, "Secret Unit Expands Rumsfeld's Domain: New Espionage Branch Delving into CIA Territory," *Washington Post*, Jan. 23, 2005, p. A1; and Douglas Jehl and Eric Schmitt, "Pentagon Seeks to Expand Role in Intelligence," *New York Times*, Dec. 19, 2004, § 1, p. 1. See also Philip Shenon, "Next Round Is Set in Push to Reorganize Intelligence," *New York Times* (late ed.), Dec. 20, 2004, p. A25.

Chapter 6

Lessons from the Organization of Intelligence in Other Countries

The 9/11 Commission's report casts only a cursory glance at foreign intelligence systems, even though some of them, notably the British, French, and Israeli, are well regarded—and those three nations have, moreover, a longer experience of dealing with terrorism than the United States.[1] That we might learn something from them seems not to have been seriously considered. In particular, the consideration the commission gave to the creation of a domestic intelligence service modeled on Britain's Security Service, more commonly known as MI5,[2]

---

1. See, for example, Jeremy Shapiro and Bénédicte Suzan, "The French Experience of Counter-Terrorism," 45 *Survival* 67 (2003). An example of the kind of study the 9/11 Commission could have consulted is Erik van de Linde et al., *Quick Scan of Post 9/11 National Counter-Terrorism Policymaking and Implementation in Selected European Countries: Research Project for the Netherlands Ministry of Justice* (RAND Europe MR-1590, May 2002).

2. "MI" stands for military intelligence, but MI5 and MI6 (the U.K.'s foreign intelligence service) have long been civilian intelligence agencies rather than components of the British armed forces. Indeed it appears that MI5 at least, despite its name, was never a military organization. A. W. Brian Simpson, *In the Highest Degree Odious: Detention without Trial in Wartime Britain* 9 (1992).

was summary,[3] indeed amateurish. Members and staff of the commission visited MI5's director-general, who told them she "doubt[ed] that such an agency could operate under the restrictions of the U.S. Constitution and the traditionally higher American emphasis on civil liberties and the right to privacy. 'Even the Brits think it wouldn't work here,' 9/11 Chairman Thomas Kean said in a news conference shortly after the commission issued its report."[4] To defer to the opinion of a foreign official concerning the limits that U.S. law and custom would place on a U.S. domestic intelligence service is absurd. It is also irrelevant, because the question is not whether such a service would have greater powers than those currently wielded by the domestic intelligence branch of the FBI but whether that branch should be separated from the FBI and made its own agency.

The commission's rejection of a U.S. MI5 was also equivocal. It said it wasn't needed *if* the commission's other recommendations were adopted.[5] Since many of them were watered down in the final version of the Intelligence Reform Act, we don't *really* know what the commission, if it still existed, would think of the idea today.

I am not suggesting that the commission or Congress should have studied the intelligence systems of all 192 foreign nations or even the systems of all major nations. Although dictatorships, for example, tend to go in for intelligence in a big way, their intelligence systems differ from those of democratic nations in ways rooted in the difference in political systems.[6]

3. *Final Report of the National Commission on Terrorist Attacks upon the United States* 423–424 (2004).

4. Scott J. Paltrow, "Secrets and Spies: U.K. Agency Makes Gains in Terror War; Can It Work Here?" *Wall Street Journal*, Oct. 6, 2004, p. A1.

5. *Final Report*, note 3 above, at 423.

6. Roy Godson, "Intelligence: An American View," in *British and American Approaches to Intelligence* 3, 6–8 (K. G. Robertson, ed., 1987).

They place greater weight on domestic relative to foreign intelligence than democracies do because they have a broader conception of subversion and because in their totalitarian form they want to control their people's thoughts rather than just their actions. They probably also engage in more extensive foreign spying; they have greater control over information and so are less likely to come to grief over leaks, and they worry less about how the public might react to embarrassing disclosures of discreditable activities. But they tend to invest less in intelligence *analysis* than democracies do because more information about open societies is publicly available, making it easier to piece together a picture of their intentions and capabilities, and because the natural insecurity of dictators makes them avid consumers of raw intelligence, Stalin being a notable example.[7]

With respect to the intelligence systems of the nations that we consider our peers in economic and political development, such as the European nations, Canada, and Japan, it would be nice to be able to conduct the kind of study I once did of the U.S. Court of Appeals for the Ninth Circuit.[8] The federal courts of appeals are divided into 13 (mainly) regional circuits. The ninth, which covers the far western states, is the largest, with 28 full-time judges, compared to 15 for the next largest. Many lawyers and judges believe that the ninth is too large, and indeed a bill recently passed the House of Representatives that would split it into three circuits. The analytical question I sought to answer was whether the ninth had grown to the point of experiencing net diseconomies of scale. I regressed performance proxies, such as summary reversals by the Supreme

7. Remarks of Oleg Tsarev, in *Agents of Change: Intelligence Services in the 21st Century* 41 (Harold Shukman, ed., 2000).
8. Richard A. Posner, "Is the Ninth Circuit Too Large? A Statistical Study of Judicial Quality," 29 *Journal of Legal Studies* 711 (2000).

Court, on circuit size, and I concluded that the ninth circuit was indeed too large. Such an approach unfortunately can't be used to evaluate a nation's intelligence system because there are no convenient performance proxies (partly because different nations face very different threats) and because the systems vary in too many ways to permit key variables to be isolated and related to the proxies. The different federal judicial circuits are more alike because they administer approximately the same body of law and are governed by the same basic procedures and the same personnel policies (for example, salaries are uniform across circuits).

Nevertheless there are two respects in which the study of foreign intelligence systems can make a constructive contribution to evaluating proposals to reform our system. First, the more closely the peer nations' systems resemble ours, the less likely it is that a radical change in our system would be an improvement. For example, our peers, like us, generally break out high-tech electronic surveillance (as distinct from wiretapping, or bugging, particular suspects) into a separate agency; thus the United Kingdom has a counterpart to the National Security Agency, which it calls the General Communications Headquarters.[9] All except Canada have a foreign intelligence agency that, like the CIA, is separate from military intelligence.[10] In the U.K., it is the Secret Intelligence Service (MI6); in France, the Direction Générale de la Sécurité Extérieur (DGSE), formerly the Service Documentation Extérieur et de

---

9. The information in this paragraph comes from a variety of sources, of which the fullest are Jeffrey T. Richelson, *Foreign Intelligence Organizations* (1988); Peter Gudgin, *Military Intelligence: A History* (1999); Paul Todd and Jonathan Bloch, *Global Intelligence: The World's Secret Services Today* (2003); and *Democracy, Law and Security: Internal Security Services in Contemporary Europe* (Jean-Paul Brodeur, Peter Gill, and Dennis Töllborg, eds., 2003).

10. Canada mainly relies on our CIA for foreign intelligence.

la Contre-Espionnage (SDECE); in Germany the Bundesnach-richtendienst (BND); in Israel the Mossad.

Our peer nations also resemble us in not folding all intelligence activities into a single agency; they rely on looser forms of coordination. The United Kingdom, for example, has a Joint Intelligence Committee on which the different agencies are represented, chaired by an official who is not affiliated with any of them. That differs from the U.S. practice before the Intelligence Reform Act, when the head of the CIA wore a second hat as Director of Central Intelligence, in which capacity he acted as the chairman of the entire intelligence community, though as I have pointed out the jobs could easily, and perhaps should, have been separated. The act has moved us in the direction of our peers by requiring that the jobs be separated and by increasing the power of the DCI (now DNI). But it has overshot the mark because the DNI is envisaged as much more powerful than a committee chairman, though how much more remains to be worked out. That none of the peer nations has a counterpart to the DNI should be a warning sign. It is an equivocal sign, because the U.S. intelligence system is much larger than that of any of those other nations and so presents a more challenging problem of control, and because only the United States has truly global reach and interests. Yet as we saw in the last chapter, usually the larger the enterprise the stronger the case for decentralization.

The second respect in which the study of foreign intelligence systems can help in evaluating proposals to reorganize our system is in identifying gaps, such as the absence of a counterpart to MI5. A domestic security agency, MI5 corresponds to the domestic intelligence service of the FBI (though it has some additional responsibilities). The task of a domestic intelligence agency is to discover plots against the nation's security that are unfolding within the nation, and thus to detect spies, saboteurs, and terrorists,[11] and to foil their plots by various means, including exposure, disinformation, "turning" an enemy operative by blackmail or bribery, and reference to prosecutorial authorities. The plots can be domestic as well as foreign; a U.S. counterpart to MI5 would keep tabs on the Ku Klux Klan and neo-Nazi organizations as well as on individuals suspected of membership in or sympathy for foreign terrorist organizations.

Like most, maybe all, intelligence services, MI5 has a checkered past. Its performance in World War II, when it utterly defeated German espionage against Britain, was outstanding, but it was run circles around by Soviet agents, such as Burgess, Maclean, Philby, and Blunt.[12] It restored its reputation in fighting the Irish Republican Army and has been praised for its work against Islamic terrorism.[13]

A U.S. counterpart to MI5 would not be a part of the Justice Department, because of the tensions between law enforcement

11. Counterintelligence, in contrast to domestic intelligence or domestic security, is concerned with preventing the penetration of the nation's intelligence services by agents of foreign powers or groups. The term is sometimes used more broadly, however, as a synonym for domestic intelligence or domestic security.

12. Peter Wright, in his book (written with Paul Greengrass) *Spy Catcher: The Candid Autobiography of a Senior Intelligence Officer* (1987), makes the sensational charge that Roger Hollis, director of MI5 from 1956 to 1965, was a Soviet agent—the fifth member of the "Cambridge Five." The charge has generally been rejected. See, for example, Anthony Glees, *The Secrets of the Service: British Intelligence and Communist Subversion 1939–51* 395 (1987); Christopher Andrew, "Unshakable Faith in Treachery," *New York Times* (late ed.), Aug. 16, 1987, § 7, p. 13. As one critic of Wright remarked, "most authorities discount Mr. Wright's charge that . . . Hollis . . . was secretly a Soviet agent. They say he was simply incompetent." Howell Raines, "In Britain, Memoir Stirs Doubt on Spy Agencies," *New York Times* (late ed.), Aug. 24, 1987, p. A2. The current belief is that John Cairncross was the fifth member. See, for example, Christopher Andrew and Vasili Mitrokhin, *The Sword and the Shield: The Mitrokhin Archive and the Secret History of the KGB* 57 (2000).

13. Paltrow, note 3 above.

and intelligence. It would either be a freestanding agency that, like the CIA, would report to the Director of National Intelligence, or it would be lodged in the Department of Homeland Security. That department corresponds to the Home Office in the U.K. (MI5 reports to the Home Secretary) and to the interior ministries in other countries.

Were there no DNI, then creating a domestic intelligence agency that, like the CIA before the Intelligence Reform Act, reported directly to the President would create acute civil liberties concerns. It would be reminiscent of Nixon's "plumbers." But creating a DNI is not a necessary response to this concern, since there is the option of placing such an agency in the Department of Homeland Security. Here I should mention that the DHS has its own intelligence service, which is a domestic intelligence service because domestic security is the department's assignment. This is a precedent for a U.S. domestic intelligence service that is not part of a police force, although a weak precedent because it is greatly overshadowed by the FBI's intelligence service. That service could be transferred to DHS and combined with the department's service. Finding a better home for a domestic intelligence service than the FBI is not the problem.

The significance of the creation of the DNI's position is that it might be thought a superior alternative to such a move. By weakening the control of the FBI director and the Attorney General over the FBI's intelligence service, the DNI might be able to integrate that service into the overall intelligence system more effectively than heretofore; the fact that the FBI's intelligence service fell outside the coordinating jurisdiction of the DCI was a weakness in the nation's intelligence setup before the Intelligence Reform Act. Yet giving the DNI a degree of control over the FBI's intelligence service seems a second-best solution to the mission incompatibility of law enforcement and intelligence. If the service should be free from the FBI's and the Justice Department's control, then transfer it to Homeland Security rather than subject it to a third master. A troika of overseers of the domestic intelligence service is a "matrix" solution (see Chapter 5) with a vengeance.

Probably most of the activities investigated by MI5 are criminal, but it is not a criminal investigation agency. It has no power of arrest. The power to arrest terrorists, spies, etc. identified by MI5 is lodged in the Special Branch of Scotland Yard; Scotland Yard is, roughly speaking, England's FBI.[14] Separating domestic intelligence from criminal investigation has advantages that I'll get to in a moment. But first I want to note the significance of the fact that every peer nation of the United States has a counterpart to MI5—the Direction de la Surveillance du Territoire (DST) in France, the Bundesamt für Verfassungsschutz (BfV) (Federal Office for the Protection of the Constitution) in Germany, Shin Bet in Israel, the Public Security Investigation Agency in Japan, the Canadian Security Intelligence Service, the Australian Security Intelligence Organisation, and so on.[15] I am not discussing some British organizational sport, such as the Duchy of Cornwall or the Confederation of the Cinque Ports. There is an international consensus that a nation's intelligence system should include a

14. Strictly, Scotland Yard is just London's plainclothes police force. The police in other parts of the United Kingdom have their own Special Branches that work with MI5. I have suppressed a number of such details (including some duties of MI5 that go beyond intelligence as ordinarily understood, such as providing security advice to private firms), which are irrelevant to my analysis.

15. Peter Chalk and William Rosenau, *Confronting the 'Enemy Within': Security Intelligence, the Police, and Counterterrorism in Four Democracies* (RAND Corp., 2004). See id. at 7–16 for a description of MI5. See also Todd Masse, "Domestic Intelligence in the United Kingdom: Applicability of the MI-5 Model to the United States: Report for Congress" (Congressional Research Service, Order Code RL31920, May 19, 2003).

domestic intelligence agency that is separate from the police. The consensus includes the nations of "old Europe" so admired by the American liberals who are in the forefront of opposition to emulating the European approach to domestic security.

We may be right and these other nations wrong. We are larger and more diverse than any of them, have a stronger civil liberties tradition, and face a wider range of threats. But the fact that we are out of step should give us pause. Some of the criticisms of creating an agency modeled on MI5 are superficial, such as that "if the Homeland Security Department and 170,000 people to be integrated is going to take a couple of years, standing up a brand new domestic intelligence agency would take a decade."[16] Or that "We're not England. We're not 500 miles across our territory. We have thousands of miles to cover. Would you propose to create an organization that had people all over the United States, as the FBI does?"[17] The Department of Homeland Security is vastly larger than the FBI, which in 2002 had only 1,644 employees on its antiterrorism staff;[18] and there is a fundamental difference between consolidating a number of heterogeneous agencies in a single agency and liberating a division from an existing agency. And although we are not England, since the core of the new agency would be the domestic intelligence service now lodged in the FBI

16. "Excerpts of Testimony from Louis J. Freeh and Janet Reno," in *The 9/11 Investigations: Staff Reports of the 9/11 Commission, Excerpts from the House-Senate Joint Inquiry Report on 9/11, Testimony from Fourteen Key Witnesses, including Richard Clarke, George Tenet, and Condoleezza Rice* 257, 264 (Steven Strasser, ed., 2004) (testimony of Freeh). The correct number of employees for the Department of Homeland Security is 180,000.

17. William Webster, quoted in U.S. Congress, Senate Select Committee on Intelligence and House Permanent Select Committee on Intelligence, *Joint Inquiry into Intelligence Community Activities before and after the Terrorist Attacks of September 11, 2001* 351 (Dec. 2002).

18. John Diamond, "CIA & FBI in the Hot Seat," *USA Today*, June 4, 2002, p. 10A.

(actually only a part of that service, as we'll see), there would be no need to create additional field staff.

What is pertinent is that our peer nations are more centralized than we; the United Kingdom, for example, has only about 50 police forces while the United States has more than 20,000. A domestic intelligence agency has to "liaise" with local law enforcement personnel—for they may turn up clues to the existence of terrorist or proto-terrorist gangs and the identity of members, sympathizers, and foreign contacts. But the creation of such an agency in this country would not require a massive duplication of the FBI's field offices, because it would be created *from* the FBI's intelligence staff. If that staff is adequate for liaison with local law enforcers, so too should the staff of the new agency be; for, initially at least, it will be largely the same staff. The creation of such an agency would involve, in the first instance at any rate, merely splitting the FBI into two (unequal) parts.

Granted, it is easier for thousands of local police departments, many quite small, to communicate with a single federal agency than with two agencies with uncertain boundaries. Uncertain because some terrorists commit quite ordinary crimes—bank robberies are a favorite method by which terrorist groups finance their activities. But the FBI and local police do not always cooperate well (that may be an understatement), in part because of a tendency of FBI agents to disdain local police, who are usually less well educated and less proficient technically, and in part because the FBI—which is, remember, a police force—is a competitor of the local police, as a domestic security agency would not be.

The remaining objection to separating out the domestic intelligence division from the FBI is that *any* reorganization is likely to disappoint. Separation should be less traumatic than merger, yet I accept the force of the objection; all reorganizations generate transition costs, and those costs may swamp the benefits, necessarily uncertain, from a reorganization of the FBI.

But it is important to see that there *would* be benefits, and they might be considerable. I pointed out in Chapter 1 that by the 9/11 Commission's own account, the FBI's domestic intelligence division, though it has the lead responsibility, certainly among intelligence services, for preventing terrorist attacks on the nation from within, turned in the most lackluster performance of any agency in protecting the nation against the activities of al Qaeda that culminated in the 9/11 attacks. (Although the attackers were foreigners, the attacks were mounted from within the United States by individuals who had been living here for months.) This failure was not an accident. Nor was it unprecedented; the FBI had failed to prevent the widespread penetration of the federal government by Soviet agents in the 1940s.

Placing the domestic intelligence function in a criminal investigation agency ensures a poor fit. Criminal investigation is retrospective. A crime has occurred and the investigators go about trying to find the criminal, and when they do they arrest him and continue gathering evidence that will be admissible in court to prove his guilt. If the criminal activity that is being investigated is of an ongoing nature, as in the case of gang acivity, the investigators may decide to allow it to continue until the activity generates irrefutable evidence of guilt. At every stage the investigator will take extreme care not to commit any procedural violation that might jeopardize a conviction. He will also be extremely reluctant to share with others any of the information that he obtains in his investigation, lest a leak tip off a suspect, or make it easier (by revealing the government's evidence) for the suspect to defend himself in court should a prosecution be instituted, or spoil the chances of a successful prosecution altogether if for example intelligence officers use the information to pressure the suspect to become a double agent. All that sharing information about a case can do from the FBI agent's perspective is weaken his ability to control the course and outcome of the case.

Thus criminal investigation is case-oriented, backward-looking, information-hugging, and fastidious (for fear of wrecking a prosecution). Domestic intelligence, in contrast, is forward-looking, threat- rather than case-oriented, and free-wheeling. Its focus is on identifying and maintaining surveillance of suspicious characters. Its preventive orientation—an orientation toward preventing crimes from occurring rather than toward prosecuting them after they occur—reduces sensitivity to avoiding a procedural misstep that might void a conviction.

Criminal investigators, because of their case orientation, can be evaluated in terms of the arrests they make, the convictions they obtain, the stolen property they recover, the sentences meted out to the criminals they apprehend. Similar output measures are unavailable for intelligence officers; they must be evaluated for promotion and compensation on an entirely different basis.[19] Furthermore, a criminal investigation agency, even one like the FBI that has a jurisdiction limited to federal crimes, has a broader subject-matter scope than a domestic intelligence agency, which is concerned with only a narrow subset of criminal activity but one that tends to unfold over a broader geographical area. There are few nationwide criminal gangs, and fewer international ones; most criminal

19. "The [FBI] rewarded agents based on statistics reflecting arrests, indictments, and prosecutions. As a result, fields such as counterterrorism and counterintelligence, where investigations generally result in fewer prosecutions, were viewed as backwaters." "Staff Statement No. 9: Law Enforcement, Counterterrorism and Intelligence Collection in the United States prior to 9/11," in *The 9/11 Investigations*, note 16 above, at 239, 241.

activity is local. This helps to explain and justify the tradition of autonomy of the FBI's field offices, and an "office of origin" mentality that treats the field office that originates a case as its owner. A reinforcing factor is that the assistant U.S. attorneys, who prosecute federal criminal cases with the FBI's assistance, are based locally rather than in Washington. In contrast, the principal domestic security danger at present emanates from international terrorist mega-gangs, and clues to their activities may be scattered all over the world.

The different orientations of the criminal investigator and the intelligence officer have implications for recruitment, retention, and promotion. Recall Kissinger's observation that "intelligence personnel in the real world are subject to unusual psychological pressures. Separated from their compatriots by security walls, operating in a culture suspicious of even unavoidable secrecy, they are surrounded by an atmosphere of cultural ambiguity. Their unadvertised and unadvertisable successes are taken for granted, while they are blamed for policies that frequently result from strategic rather than intelligence misjudgments." This does not sound like the description of an FBI agent, and it casts doubt on the value of the FBI's post-9/11 program of providing intelligence training to its criminal investigators. "The worlds of law enforcement and intelligence are far apart. They have different roles, different rules, and different cultures, and often they do not speak the same language."[20]

The fundamental objection to assigning seriously disparate missions to the same agency is the "uniformitarian" problem that I discussed in the last chapter. The effective control of an organization requires imposing some minimum uniformity in compensation, recruitment, evaluation, promotion, and work-

20. Elizabeth Rindskopf, "Comment," in *U.S. Intelligence at the Crossroads: Agendas for Reform* 256 (Roy Godson, Ernest R. May, and Gary Schmitt, eds., 1995).

ing conditions in order to minimize conflict, foster cooperation, and avoid confusion and uncertainty. If the missions assigned to the organization are too disparate—if their optimal performance requires radically different approaches, personnel, and so forth—then the compromise necessary to impose the requisite minimum uniformity may cause many of the missions to be performed poorly. (If shoes came in only one size, they would be cheap to manufacture but most people would be poorly shod.) That is the likely fate of the FBI's intelligence mission. It makes it difficult for the Bureau to compete with the CIA for first-rate intelligence officers as well as to get the best results from its officers.

The current director has vowed to change the culture of the FBI. But what can that mean exactly? The FBI cannot change itself into an intelligence agency, because an intelligence agency cannot conduct criminal investigations over the entire range of federal crimes. It will remain a hybrid agency, though at best one with a strong domestic intelligence service coexisting uneasily with a strong criminal-investigation service. But this seems unlikely too. It is terribly difficult for the head of an established government agency, especially one brought in from the outside, to change the agency's culture. It is only three and a half years since 9/11, which means that most of the FBI's professional employees, including those at the senior levels, are holdovers from the ancien régime. They are unlikely to welcome the transformative moves being attempted by Director Mueller; and civil servants are adept at passive resistance.

The marriage of criminal investigation and domestic intelligence in the FBI also complicates the coordination of domestic and foreign intelligence. The threats to internal security that seem at the moment most ominous have foreign origins, and as a consequence often the same suspects are tracked outside the United States by the CIA and inside by the FBI's intelligence division. Yet the CIA and FBI have a history of mutual suspicion and antipathy.[21] This had begun to diminish even before 9/11, especially at the top of the two agencies. But the cultural and procedural gulf between criminal investigations and intelligence operations remains, and it impairs coordination between the two agencies just as it does within the FBI. Coordination is made still more awkward by the fact that the FBI's intelligence service is under the direction not just of the FBI director but, above him, of the Attorney General, who is the nation's chief legal officer and may therefore be uncomfortable with the methods employed by an intelligence agency, since they press against the legal limits of investigation and surveillance.

That the FBI's criminal investigation activity will continue to overshadow its intelligence activity is signaled by the Reform Act's designation of the Bureau's intelligence director as the "Executive Assistant Director for Intelligence of the Federal Bureau of Investigation."[22] In the federal pecking order, an executive assistant director is a very small bird. FBI intelligence officers will be reporting to an assistant (not deputy) director who is at many removes from the President.

The Reform Act did something else in this line that is more troubling. Before the act, the FBI's Office of Intelligence was responsible mainly for training and recruitment, but not for operations, which were the responsibility of the Bureau's Counterterrorism Division. The act redesignates the Office of Intelligence as the Directorate of Intelligence and assigns it a variety of important tasks, including "supervision of all national

21. See, for example, Mark Riebling, *Wedge: The Secret War between the FBI and the CIA* (1994).

22. Intelligence Reform and Terrorism Prevention Act of 2004, Title II, § 2002(b).

intelligence programs, projects, and activities of the Bureau."[23] The act does not mention the Counterterrorism Division, so that the Bureau's intelligence service is to remain split between two divisions, with the Directorate of Intelligence corresponding to the CIA's Directorate of Intelligence (the analytic branch) and the Counterterrorism Division, which does not report to the new Executive Assistant for Intelligence, corresponding to the CIA's Directorate of Operations. This means that the FBI does not have *a* domestic intelligence service, but instead two services that have domestic intelligence responsibilities—and criminal-investigation responsibilities to boot. For the Directorate of Intelligence is not limited to intelligence concerning threats to national security; it includes intelligence about ordinary criminal activities within the Bureau's jurisdiction. And the Counterterrorism Division is engaged in arresting and gathering evidence for prosecuting terrorists, as well as in MI5-type antiterrorist activities, for remember that MI5 has no arrest power or prosecutorial functions. So three and a half years after 9/11, the Bureau *still* has not separated domestic intelligence from criminal investigation; what I have been calling the FBI's domestic intelligence service remains both split and deeply entangled with criminal investigations. This makes it difficult even to gauge the Bureau's commitment to MI5-type domestic intelligence activity.

In the unlikely event that the intelligence branch of the FBI should ever come to overshadow the criminal-investigation branch, the civil libertarians will have a fit, for once justified. The only sure way to prevent either branch from overshadowing the other is to separate out the intelligence branch into a new agency.

MI5 and MI6 work well together (as far as I can judge).

23. Id., § 2002(c)(1).

Both are, after all, intelligence agencies, although the centralization of English government and society in London, and the homogeneity of the English governing class, must help bind the agencies to each other. The FBI has tended not to work well with the CIA because, as I have been emphasizing, it is not an intelligence agency. Granted, a domestic intelligence agency must coordinate its activities with the nation's criminal investigation agencies as well as with its foreign intelligence agency, because criminal prosecutions are an important tool of domestic security. MI5 has some of the same problems coordinating with the Special Branch of Scotland Yard that the CIA has coordinating with the FBI;[24] a U.S. domestic security agency modeled on MI5 would encounter similar problems. But a section of the FBI that like the Special Branch was specialized to the arrest and prosecution of terrorists would make a better fit with a domestic intelligence agency modeled on MI5 than the FBI's domestic intelligence service makes with the rest of the FBI. The focus of the FBI will always be on criminal investigation, not only as a matter of tradition and organizational culture but also because (one hopes) ordinary crime fighting will always require greater resources than domestic intelligence; there is more crime than there is terrorism, and it is costly to prepare a criminal prosecution. So intelligence officers lodged in the FBI are likely to remain the odd men out.

But while a person wanting a career in intelligence will not be attracted to working for a police department, it is different with someone wanting a career in the criminal investigation and prosecution of terrorists—a prestigious and exciting field of police work. Such a unit in the FBI, which would correspond to Scotland Yard's Special Branch, could hold its head high and

24. In the words of a former officer of MI5, there are "definite tensions between the two organizations: Special Branch would like to be us, and we don't want to be them." Wright, note 12 above, at 32.

would at the same time have a strong incentive to cooperate with a domestic intelligence agency because that agency would be the source of most of the unit's prosecutions.

Speaking of mission incompatibilities, it might seem logical, should a domestic intelligence agency be created, to shift the CIA's counterintelligence branch to it because of the tension that I noted in the preceding chapter between the CIA's intelligence and counterintelligence branches. Just as the criminal investigation side of the FBI dominates the Bureau, so the intelligence side of the CIA dominates the agency. Counterintelligence officers may be led to pull their punches because a person suspected of being a mole may be one of the agency's valued officers. But such a separation would probably be a bad idea. The reason is that counterintelligence officers are most likely to learn about a penetration from the intelligence officers in their own service. CIA intelligence officers may for example discover that one of the agency's spies in Russia thinks that Russia has a mole in the CIA, and at least until their suspicions are confirmed they will be far more reluctant to share those suspicions with outsiders than with the CIA's own counterintelligence officers.

I have mentioned what seem to me the major objections to creating a U.S. counterpart to MI5: that it would complicate the communication network that connects the FBI to thousands of police departments and that most government reorganizations fail and even if they succeed impose substantial transition costs. A less weighty objection is that creating a new agency would intensify the problem of controlling the intelligence system by increasing the number of separate intelligence agencies, as in Senator Roberts's proposal except that the number would increase by one rather than by three. But there would be no real increase, because the FBI's intelligence division is currently one of the nation's intelligence services and must be coordinated with the others. Indeed, it is so important a one that the 9/11 Commission recommended that its head be eligible to be one of three Deputy Directors of National Intelligence. What would be mainly involved in the creation of an MI5-type agency would be separating the FBI's intelligence service (or rather the part of it that does not work on ordinary crimes) from a criminal investigation division that is not an intelligence service. And while the unit in the criminal investigation division that is responsible for actually prosecuting security-related crimes would have to coordinate its work with that of the intelligence service, it would not have to participate in and thus complicate the higher-level coordination of the nation's intelligence services.

Another objection is that since we can live (*pace* Senator Roberts) with the tensions created by lodging clandestine intelligence operations, counterintelligence, technical intelligence gathering, and intelligence analysis all in one agency (the CIA), we should be able to live with the joinder of criminal investigation and domestic intelligence in the FBI. But the incompatibility is greater in the case of the FBI. The four services that are combined in the CIA all have the same mission, that of obtaining accurate assessments of the intentions and capabilities of foreign enemies, actual or potential, whether states or, like al Qaeda, nonstate entities. The missions of the criminal investigative and domestic intelligence branches of the FBI are different, as I have been emphasizing. One is concerned with apprehending the full range of violators of federal crimes, the other with preventing (and not through punishment, but through exposure, disinformation, bribery, cajolery, threats, and other nonprosecutorial means) espionage, sabotage, and other acts inimical to national security. The missions are not only different; to a great extent they are incompatible.

They are not, however, *entirely* incompatible, which suggests another objection to splitting them apart. Criminal investigators can assist in the core functions of a domestic intelligence agency; for example, arrests can be used to extract information from a person or to turn him, as by threatening to tell his accomplices that he is cooperating with the authorities. Also, criminal investigators have clear criteria for what constitutes proof rather than mere grounds for suspicion, and familiarity with those criteria might prevent intelligence operatives from going off on wild goose chases. But this is just to say that a background in criminal investigation would be something a domestic intelligence service would want some of its employees to have, which is different from having the service lodged in an agency that is headed by a judge or a prosecutor (the current FBI director is a former prosecutor, his immediate predecessor was a former judge, the judge's immediate predecessor was a prosecutor, and *his* immediate predecessor was another judge) and that conceives its principal mission to be the investigation and prosecution of the full range of federal crimes.

But the real deal breaker is the fear that a domestic intelligence agency, torn free from the legalistic culture of the FBI (of the post–J. Edgar Hoover FBI, that is to say), would endanger civil liberties. The history of MI5 furnishes evidence to support that fear.[25] One of its former officers has said that "MI5 operated on the basis of the 11th Commandment—'Thou shalt not get caught.'"[26] The past tense may be significant, however. Although England may have invented civil liberties, until recently they received much less protection than in the United

25. See, in particular, Simpson, note 2 above; also Paltrow, note 3 above.
26. Wright, note 12 above, at 31.

States. MI5 operated with many fewer legal restrictions than the domestic intelligence service of the FBI does—though the comparison is misleading. Legal restrictions on the FBI's freedom of action that may well have been too strict and that have been progressively relaxed under Republican Presidents beginning with Reagan had been imposed in reaction to the Bureau's excesses in domestic security matters involving Communists and other left-wing radicals. Those excesses, which persisted until the early 1970s, resemble the abuses by MI5 that Professor Simpson recounts in his history of domestic repression in the U.K. during World War II.[27]

As part of a trend toward greater protection of civil liberties in the United Kingdom,[28] MI5 has become more temperate in the use of its powers, though it remains freer of legal, and in particular judicial, control than the FBI. It can, for example, conduct wiretaps and searches without judicial approval, though there is provision for review by an impartial administrative tribunal.[29] But these are details; a U.S. counterpart to MI5 could be required to obtain authorization for wiretaps and searches from the Foreign Intelligence Surveillance Court (presumably renamed to drop "Foreign" from its title), which exercises such authority with respect to wiretaps and searches of persons in the United States (other than citizens) who have links to suspect foreign groups.[30] Indeed, some degree of judi-

27. Simpson, note 2 above.

28. Dramatically illustrated by the recent decision of the House of Lords invalidating a post-9/11 law allowing indefinite detention, without a hearing, of aliens suspected of terrorism who could not be deported because either no nation would accept them or only a nation in which they would be exposed to torture or other serious harms. *A v. Secretary of State*, [2004] UKHL 56, [2004] All ER(D) 271 (Dec. 26, 2004).

29. Todd and Bloch, note 9 above, at 102–105; Michael Supperstone, "The Law Relating to Security in Great Britain," in *British and American Approaches to Intelligence*, note 6 above, at 218, 223.

30. 50 U.S.C. §§ 1801 *et seq*. "Groups," not just "foreign powers." And as I

cial oversight of a domestic intelligence agency would be implicit in the fact that the agency's employees could be sued for violating constitutional rights, for example the right of free speech conferred by the First Amendment or the right to be free from unreasonable searches and seizures conferred by the Fourth.

Yet such an agency doubtless would strain more at the constitutional leash than the FBI, which has to worry not only about endangering convictions directly but also about inviting judicial criticism that could have an indirect adverse effect on convictions. Not being part of a criminal investigation agency, less likely to be dominated by lawyers, not lodged in the Department of Justice, not as often before a court, and not oriented toward prosecutions, a domestic intelligence service would worry less than the FBI and the entire Justice Department do about angering civil libertarians. Consider an investigative project such as dispatching an undercover agent to a public meeting of a Muslim political group in order to identify participants and make a record of what is said at the meeting, and perhaps following up by compiling dossiers on some of the participants or even by assigning undercover agents to join the group to spy on it or disrupt its activities by feeding it with false information. Such activity, at least until it reaches the stage of disruption, is not unlawful.[31] But it disturbs civil libertarians because it makes people more cautious about what they say publicly and so impairs the vigor of political debate. A domestic intelligence agency the principal mission of which was to detect and disrupt subversive conspiracies in their incipience,

---

noted in Chapter 2, the Intelligence Reform Act has extended the coverage of the Foreign Intelligence Surveillance Act to persons (provided they are not citizens) who are suspected of terrorism but are not working for or on behalf of a foreign nation or group, but instead are lone wolves.

31. See, for example, *Alliance to End Repression v. City of Chicago*, 356 F.3d 767 (7th Cir. 2004).

rather than let them fester until they generated rich evidence for a criminal prosecution, would be less sensitive to civil libertarians' concerns than a law enforcement agency intent on making criminal convictions stick and concerned therefore to retain the goodwill of the judiciary, which tends to take a proprietary interest in defendants' rights.

Yet one doubts whether the creation of a domestic intelligence service modeled on MI5 would actually result in a net reduction in the scope of Americans' civil liberties. Although the FBI's domestic intelligence service is unlikely ever to dominate the FBI, let alone the Justice Department as a whole, it could conceivably dilute the Bureau's and the department's commitment to civil liberties. And as far as contamination of ordinary law enforcement by intelligence activities is concerned, the cat may be out of the bag. The Director of National Intelligence will be exercising authority over the FBI's domestic intelligence service. This means that the same official will be the overseer of both foreign and domestic intelligence—and on this ground the American Civil Liberties Union opposed the creation of the position.[32] The *incremental* effect on civil liberties of extruding domestic intelligence from the FBI may therefore be slight or even nonexistent.

In any event, the fact that such a change might result in some reduction in the scope of civil liberties is not a decisive argument against the change. Civil liberties are important. They may well be important enough to justify sacrificing the undoubted efficiencies that would be reaped by combining domestic and foreign intelligence in the same agency: the fear is that the agency would treat domestic enemies with as little

32. American Civil Liberties Union, "Civil Liberties and the 9/11 Commission: An ACLU White Paper on Notable Findings and Recommendations in the Final Report of the National Commission on Terrorist Attacks Upon the United States" (Aug. 3, 2004), at www.aclu.org/Files/OpenFile.cfm?id 6203.

consideration for their rights or interests as it treats foreign enemies. But like other goods, civil liberties should be subject to trade-offs rather than being fetishized as the ACLU is prone to do. The term "civil liberties" merely denotes the point of balance between society's interests in liberty and in security.[33] As the weights of these interests change with altered circumstances, the balance shifts. In wartime the interest in security soars and so civil liberties are diminished; and our current struggle with international terrorism is, like the Cold War, plausibly described as war.

The idea of trading off civil liberties against national security is resisted on a number of grounds. Geoffrey Stone argues that history shows that we place too much weight on security. "The United States has a long and unfortunate history of overreacting to the dangers of wartime."[34] The point, even if true (I think it is largely though not entirely true), and even disregarding the fact that measures may be prudent even if hindsight reveals that they weren't really necessary, is less compelling than Stone believes. It assumes a degree of precision in responding to threats that is unattainable as a practical matter. Public policy is a crude instrument of social control. Fine-tuning is not an art of government; the tendency is for policy to swing from one dumb extreme to the other. The realistic choice in responding to the threat of Soviet espionage and subversion during the Cold War was not between the optimal response and overreaction but between underreaction and overreaction, and the former might have been more dangerous.

Another objection to allowing civil liberties to expand and

33. Richard A. Posner, *Law, Pragmatism, and Democracy* 293–317 (2003); Posner, *Catastrophe: Risk and Response* 224–243 (2004).
34. Geoffrey R. Stone, *Perilous Times: Free Speech in Wartime: From the Sedition Act of 1798 to the War on Terrorism* 528 (2004).

contract with changes in the security situation is that reductions in civil liberties in wartime may not be restored when the war ends. So if such reductions are permitted, a succession of wars may produce an uninterrupted decline in civil liberties. Stone rejects this objection. He notes that not only have civil liberties been fully restored after each of our wars, but the overall trend in protecting civil liberties has been upward.[35] But he adds that "in periods of relative calm the [Supreme] Court should consciously construct constitutional doctrines that will provide firm and unequivocal guidance for later periods of stress."[36] That sounds like tying the government's hands in wartime. And while he acknowledges that the scope of civil liberties is, in the end, a matter of balancing liberty and security,[37] he does so grudgingly, for he adds: "I concede that security is as 'important' as liberty, though I am not quite sure what that means."[38] He may think it always possible to offset the negative effect of expansive civil liberties on national security by investing more in defensive measures. But he doesn't say this, and it is unclear that it is so — or that he would favor massive increases in defense spending as an alternative to a modest curtailment of civil liberties.

Civil libertarians question the applicability of the "rebound" thesis to the current struggle against international terrorism on the ground that the struggle has no natural terminus; if it will never end, the reduction in civil liberties in response to it will be permanent. But the fact that the end of a war cannot be foreseen doesn't mean that it will last forever; no wars have

35. Id. at 530–531, 533, 548–549, 551.
36. Id. at 548.
37. Id. at 546.
38. Id. at 547. My guess is that Professor Stone was less insouciant about personal security back when conservatives were saying, "Better dead than Red."

lasted forever. The Cold War lasted more than 40 years, and who can say that the current war against Islamist terrorism will last as long or longer?

Although Stone doesn't make the mistake of confusing the indefinite with the infinite, he does argue that "a war of indefinite duration . . . compounds the dangers [created by restricting civil liberties] both by extending the period during which civil liberties are 'suspended' and by increasing the risk that 'emergency' restrictions will become a permanent fixture of American life."[39] In saying this he ignores the history recounted at such length in his book, which shows that restrictions on civil liberties are greatest at the outset of an emergency and rapidly dwindle, often to nothing, before the war ends. Most of Lincoln's suspensions of habeas corpus occurred at the outset of the Civil War; the gravest infringement of civil liberties in World War II—the internment of West Coast Japanese Americans—occurred pursuant to an order issued just a few months after Pearl Harbor; although the Cold War lasted from 1947 to 1989, the anticommunist excesses of which Stone complains were concentrated in the first decade and by the early 1960s had abated completely even though the Cold War still had a quarter century to run; and the measures taken in response to 9/11 (most dramatically, the suspension for several days of all civil aviation) have also abated, though not yet completely.

This time pattern of restrictions on civil liberties is not happenstance. When a nation is attacked, there is at first great uncertainty about the gravity of the attack, so naturally and sensibly the government responds with severe measures. The longer the struggle initiated by the attack continues, the more accurate the assessment of danger becomes, and so it becomes

39. Id. at 554–555.

possible to scale back the repressive measures—and they *are* scaled back, as the history recounted by Stone teaches. The harsher the initial measures, moreover, the sooner the period of repression ends. One reason the anticommunist "hysteria" had abated by the beginning of the 1960s is that the measures that Stone deplores had succeeded in rooting Communists and their sympathizers out of the government and indeed crushing the entire communist movement in the United States.[40] By the end of the Eisenhower administration there was little fear— because there was little basis for fear—of communist subversion in the United States.

Curtailment of civil liberties in times of danger is also resisted on the ground that the harm to innocent people exceeds the benefit in greater security. This point implicitly accepts a balancing approach to determining the scope of civil liberties but on the civil liberties side of the balance adds to the loss of rather abstract goods, such as unfettered freedom of speech, the suffering of the people who lose their jobs or suffer some other tangible loss. At the abstract level the case for unrestricted civil liberties in wartime is particularly thin and unconvincing. Although total curtailment of civil liberties would indeed create a climate of fear and silence criticism of government policies and officials, the modest curtailments imposed by the U.S. government in wartime, including both the Cold War and the current struggle against international terrorism, have not had that effect. Could anyone argue with a straight face that the USA PATRIOT Act or the other much-criticized police measures adopted in the wake of the 9/11 attacks intimidated opposition to the war in Iraq or dampened the vigor of the 2004 Presidential election campaign?

40. Robert Louis Benson and Michael Warner, "Preface," in *Venona: Soviet Espionage and the American Response, 1939–1957* vii, xxix–xxx (Benson and Warner, eds., 1996).

But at the retail level, as it were, wartime police measures, including purely private acts of persecution inspired by them (such as the blacklisting of left-wing writers, directors, and actors by the Hollywood studios during the 1950s), can impose demonstrable harms on specific individuals. Think of the financial and dignitary harms suffered by the many thousands of Japanese Americans interned after Pearl Harbor in the mistaken belief that they were disloyal, and the humiliation, fear, discomfort, and physical pain experienced by the torture victims at Abu Ghraib. But although the full range of costs imposed by a curtailment of civil liberties should be weighed in the balance, it doesn't follow that they will always preponderate. That depends on the measures under consideration. An American MI5 would not be authorized to assassinate or to torture, or even to arrest, intern, or deport. But its activities—its very existence—would intimidate some people and invade the privacy of others (at the same time that it would symbolize a national determination to take terrorism with the seriousness that it deserves). And the agency's operatives would sometimes cross the line and commit illegal acts. It doesn't follow that the aggregate costs would exceed the benefits, given the dangers that the nation faces from terrorism (of which more in the Conclusion), even if, as I doubt, the creation of such an agency would result in a *net* increase in abuses.

The last objection to any curtailment of civil liberties in times of danger is the most tenacious, because it is based not on practical concerns but on ideology. Although there are conservative opponents of curtailing civil liberties even slightly (some found on the radical right, with its paranoid distrust of government), the vast majority of the opponents are liberals in the modern (not the John Stuart Mill) sense of the word. And a defining mark of the modern liberal is an instinctive hostility to the police and the military, and more broadly to governmental use of force both internally and externally, and an abiding belief that threats to national security, especially when they emanate from left-wing regimes or groups, or from non-Western or formerly colonized nations, are systematically exaggerated.

The most recent example of this outlook is Lord Hoffmann's opinion in the House of Lords case that I cited earlier.[41] Noting that "the power which the Home Secretary seeks to uphold is a power to detain people indefinitely without charge or trial," Hoffmann says that "nothing could be more antithetical to the instincts and traditions of the people of the United Kingdom." Hardly; for this ignores among other things the abuses by MI5; and Hoffmann quickly adds that the draconian laws enacted to crush the Irish Republican Army, laws similar to those enacted after 9/11, were justifiable because "it was reasonable to say that terrorism in Northern Ireland threatened the life of that part of the nation and the territorial integrity of the United Kingdom as a whole." But while acknowledging that "the threat of similar atrocities"—similar, that is, to the 9/11 attacks—"in the United Kingdom is a real one," Hoffmann denies that it is "a threat to the life of the nation. . . . Whether we would survive Hitler hung in the balance, but there is no doubt that we shall survive Al-Qaeda." Actually, there is more doubt that the United Kingdom will survive Islamic terrorism than there was that it would survive the Irish Republican Army, the aims of which were modest compared to those of Osama Bin Laden and his associates and which did not aspire to possess weapons of mass destruction. Hoffman adds that "terrorist violence, serious as it is, does not threaten our institutions of government." But considering how fiercely the British author-

41. The quotations that follows are from pp. 29–31 of the opinion, note 28 above.

ities responded to the 9/11 attacks on the United States, one imagines that their response to a similar or worse attack on Britain would leave little of the institutional framework of civil liberties standing.

Hoffmann concludes with a rhetorical flourish that epitomizes the ideological approach to civil liberties: "The real threat to the life of the nation, in the sense of a people living in accordance with its traditional laws and political values, comes not from terrorism but from laws such as these. That is the true measure of what terrorism may achieve. It is for Parliament to decide whether to give the terrorists such a victory." In short, terrorism is not a "real threat," but the enactments of a democratic legislature ("laws such as these") are. Terrorism that kills thousands of people (in time, it could be tens of thousands or hundreds of thousands, or even millions) is as nothing compared to laws that cut back on "traditional laws and political values," even if the "traditions" are only a few years old. Ordinary sensible people don't take the prospect of mass murder so lightly or doubt that terrorism on the scale enabled by modern technology and inflamed by religio-political fanaticism can do more harm than a law authorizing the indefinite detention of nondeportable aliens (a total of 17) suspected of being terrorists.

A less extreme tendency to belittle threats to national security is on display in Stone's book, notably in his discussion of the antisubversive measures that the United States employed during the Cold War. Although he acknowledges communist "espionage against the government of the United States,"[42] he leaves out the details that would enable the reader to gauge its scope and consequences.[43] No estimate is offered of the num-

42. Stone, note 34 above, at 409–410.
43. See, for example, *Venona*, note 40 above; Katherine L. Herbig and Martin F. Wiskoff, *Espionage against the United States by American Citizens 1947–*

ber of Soviet spies in the United States and allied nations (notably Britain and West Germany). The guilt of Alger Hiss,[44] a high official, is not explicitly acknowledged, or that of Lauchlin Currie, an assistant to President Roosevelt; and the Rosenbergs are described as *"alleged conspirators."*[45] Stone acknowledges in a footnote that "according to some researchers," in 1945 an assistant secretary of the Treasury (Harry Dexter White) was a Soviet agent.[46] But the qualification "according to some researchers" introduces an unjustified note of dubiety,[47] and the text invites the reader to sympathize with White, who, "suffering from a weak heart, and 'emotionally outraged' by the humiliation of his experience . . . died three days after his testimony [before the House Un-American Activities Committee]."[48] Yet it was White himself who "insisted on appearing personally before [the committee]."[49]

Stone does not remark the existence of "major Soviet espi-

2001 (Defense Personnel Security Research Center [PERSEREC], Technical Report 02-5, July 2002), and references cited in id. at 2 4. "Wartime cooperation between these uneasy allies [the United States and the Soviet Union] allowed Soviet intelligence to dig into the burgeoning bureaucracy in Washington, where its recruits swelled from dozens in the late 1930s to several hundred during the war. According to transcripts of Soviet wartime cables deciphered by the National Security Agency (NSA) in the *Venona* project, codenames of some 350 cooperating Americans appear in Soviet wartime cable traffic. The finest hour for Soviet intelligence gathering during the war came with the penetration of the secret Manhattan project by the atom spy ring, Julius and Ethel Rosenberg, Klaus Fuchs, and their associates." Id. at 5.

44. Allen Weinstein, *Perjury: The Hiss-Chambers Case* (1978); John Earl Haynes and Harvey Klehr, *Venona: Decoding Soviet Espionage in America* 167–173 (1999).

45. Stone, note 34 above, at 331 (emphasis added).

46. Id. at 368 n.*.

47. Christopher Andrew, "Intelligence in the Cold War: Lessons and Learning," in *Agents for Change: Intelligence Services in the 21st Century* 1, 7 (Harold Shukman, ed., 2000).

48. Stone, note 34 above, at 368.

49. Id. at 368 n.*.

onage rings—which included employees of the OSS, War Department, War Production Board, Foreign Economic Administration, and the Treasury, Agriculture, and Commerce departments."[50] The Venona tapes, which belatedly revealed the extent of Soviet penetration of the U.S. government,[51] go unmentioned as well, along with the subservience of the U.S. Communist Party to the Soviet-controlled Communist International (Comintern).[52]

Stone's treatment of the outbreak of the Korean War is revealing:

> Early on Sunday morning, June 25, 1950, North Korean artillery opened fire on South Korean army positions south of the thirty-eighth parallel, the line dividing Communist North Korea from the Republic of South Korea. The opening barrage was followed by intense tank and infantry attacks at all points along the parallel. Within days, the UN Security Council called upon member nations to give military aid to South Korea and President Truman authorized General Douglas MacArthur to invade North Korea.[53]

Stone does not say that North Korea invaded South Korea. He says that North Korean artillery fired on South Korean army positions (as if the two nations were *already* at war), and that this was followed by "attacks," implicitly by North Korea but he does not actually say so. There is no mention of the Soviet Union, which had armed North Korea and encouraged the invasion. The only mention of an invasion is that within a few days of the outbreak of the war Truman authorized MacArthur to "invade" North Korea. Ignored is the fact that MacArthur had

50. Jeffrey T. Richelson, *A Century of Spies: Intelligence in the Twentieth Century* 225 (1995); Haynes and Klehr, note 44 above.

51. Id.; *Venona*, note 40 above.

52. Harvey Klehr, John Earl Haynes, and Kyrill M. Anderson, *The Soviet World of American Communism* (1998).

53. Stone, note 34 above, at 334.

to fight a desperate rearguard action for months before he could go on the attack and eventually cross the border into North Korea.

Immediately after the quoted passage the reader is told that "the outbreak of the Korean War unleashed a frenzy of anti-Red hysteria. Republican rhetoric, reminiscent of Federalist charges in 1798, reached fever pitch."[54] Stone does not mention that the Korean War, an act of naked communist aggression, was widely believed to be a possible overture to World War III, intended to distract the United States from a Soviet invasion of western Europe.[55] So it is hardly surprising that the Korean War provoked a strong reaction in the United States against communism—a reaction that was not limited to Republicans. In suggesting that it was, Stone plays into the hands of today's Republicans, who accuse the Democrats of being weak on security issues.

The language in which Stone describes the reaction to North Korea's invasion of South Korea—"frenzy," "anti-Red hysteria," "fever pitch"—obscures the genuine grounds for concern about Soviet espionage and subversion. A particular irony is that the McCarthyite excesses that followed the invasion can be traced, in part at least, to the atom spies, who accelerated the Soviet Union's acquisition of the atomic bomb. The acqui-

54. Id.

55. Gordon Rottman, *Korean War Order of Battle: United States, United Nations, and Community Ground, Naval and Air Forces, 1950–1953* 4 (2002); Carter Malkasian, *The Korean War: 1950–1953* 73 (2001); Robert Leckie, *Conflict: The History of the Korean War, 1950–1953* 53 (1962); James I. Matray, "Truman's Plan for Victory: National Self-Determination and the Thirty-Eighth Parallel Decision in Korea," 66 *Journal of American History* 314, 318 (1979); Samuel F. Wells, Jr., "Sounding the Tocsin: NSC 68 and the Soviet Union," 4 *International Security* 116, 132, 140 (1979); Tracy S. Voorhees, "To Prevent a 'Korea' in Western Europe: A Full-Scale Build-Up of Atlantic Pact Allies Is Urged to Discourage Soviet Aggression," *New York Times Magazine*, July 23, 1950, p. 10.

sition may have emboldened Stalin to challenge the United States by encouraging North Korea to invade South Korea.[56] At least that is what Judge Irving Kaufman believed when he sentenced the Rosenbergs to death. I consider the sentence excessive. But part of the blame falls on the lax security measures that enabled the Soviet Union to obtain information vital to its atomic program. Such are the consequences of a regard for civil liberties that lacks nuance and balance.

In summary, the 9/11 Commission and its congressional followers were too hasty in rejecting out of hand the idea of creating a domestic intelligence service outside the FBI. The obstacles to creating such an agency are formidable, and though some are based on politics and defense of turf[57] others have substance. As an outsider to national security issues, I lack the knowledge and experience that would justify my tak-

56. Haynes and Klehr, note 44 above, at 11; John Earl Haynes, *Red Scare or Red Menace? American Communism and Anticommunism in the Cold War Era* 63 (1996). For a skeptical view, see William Stueck, *Rethinking the Korean War: A New Diplomatic and Strategic History* 73 (2002); Michael E. Parrish, "Review Essay: Soviet Espionage and the Cold War," 25 *Diplomatic History* 105, 117 (2001).

57. These obstacles have been well described by Richard Clarke: "The reality in America is that there are two hurdles to the creation of a new, effective security service. The first is the right-left political alliance against security measures and the second is the FBI itself. The right-left political alliance is the phenomenon in which organizations like the National Rifle Association and the American Civil Liberties Union come together, usually with congressmen like Dick Armey, to express concern at efforts to strengthen the hand of domestic security officials. Any legislation proposing a security service will be met by a barrage of critics before they even read the bill. The FBI, which does not want to lose the domestic security mission to some new agency, will also work hard in the media and the Congress to scuttle any legislation. Were the legislation to pass, many FBI personnel will display passive-aggressive behavior rather than assist or cooperate with the security service." Richard A. Clarke, *Against All Enemies: Inside America's War on Terror* 255 (2004).

ing a firm position pro or con the creation of such an agency. All that I can say—but this with some confidence—is that the question merits a fuller airing than Congress or the 9/11 Commission gave it in the deliberations that resulted in the Intelligence Reform Act.

Conclusion

What Is to Be Done?

I have offered no blueprint for the organization of our intelligence system, whether within or outside the framework created by the Intelligence Reform and Terrorism Prevention Act of 2004 (a loose framework, I have argued). My effort has been to evaluate, in the light of logic and common sense plus the publicly available materials bearing on the Issue, the case made by the 9/11 Commission and other proponents of reorganizing the system so as to centralize control more than has been the tradition. I have found the case to be unconvincing; indeed, it has barely been made, whether in the commission's report or elsewhere. This is no surprise when one considers the errors in the composition of the commission, the timing of its report, the precipitate reaction of the Presidential candidates, the stampede in Congress, and the laxity of the media.

It was the political equivalent of a plane crash. Because of the redundancy of its components (and here is another example of why duplication need not be "wasteful"), a plane is very unlikely to crash unless there is a sequence of component failures. And similarly a piece of legislation as dangerously bad as the structural provisions of the Intelligence Reform Act is unlikely to be enacted unless all the usual barriers to the over-hasty enactment of complex, ill-considered legislation collapse at once. As appears to have happened, the last straw being the assignment of the Senate bill to the Governmental Affairs Committee rather than to a committee that focuses on intelligence or national security matters.

The disconnect between the commission's narrative of the events of, preceding, and immediately following the terrorist attacks of September 11, 2001, and the organizational recommendations tucked in the back of the commission's report, is complete, as is the commission's apparent neglect to consult the studies in a variety of scholarly fields that bear on the question of how to organize a nation's intelligence system. In responding, prematurely and hastily, to the commission's proposal, Congress did not plug the gaps in the commission's analysis or rectify the deficiencies in the commission's organizational recommendations. The Intelligence Reform Act is a backward step in the reform of the U.S. intelligence system.

Seconded by Congress, the commission summarily rejected the structural change most clearly implied not only by its own narrative of the events behind the failure to prevent the 9/11 attacks but also by the various literatures that I have reviewed in this book: removing the FBI's intelligence service from the Bureau and making it the nucleus of a domestic intelligence agency modeled on the United Kingdom's MI5 and similar organizations in other countries. One reason for that summary rejection, I speculate, is that the commission was unwilling to grapple with the sensitive issue, which I discussed at the end of the last chapter, of trading off liberty against security. For it is widely, though quite possibly incorrectly, believed that a domestic intelligence agency would weaken civil liberties beyond what has been done by the USA PATRIOT Act as amplified by similar antiterrorist provisions in the Intelligence

Reform Act. But perhaps a future Congress will return to the issue of creating a U.S. MI5; indeed, a tiny silver lining in the structural provisions of the Intelligence Reform Act is that the advent of an official (the Director of National Intelligence) with responsibility for domestic as well as foreign intelligence alleviates concern that a freestanding domestic security agency, reporting only to the President, would be a threat to civil liberties.

Another sensible structural change, not unrelated to what the Reform Act has done but far more modest, might have been to separate the positions of Director of Central Intelligence and Director of the Central Intelligence Agency. That would have freed up the DCI to concentrate on coordinating the components of the national intelligence system, with particular reference to the agencies responsible for the high-tech methods of intelligence and to the interface between domestic and foreign intelligence. He not only would have had the time to play such a coordinating role, but would have been unburdened by the conflict of interest inherent in managing one intelligence agency while supervising the coordination of all the agencies.

The structural changes that the commission did propose, and that Congress enacted, are not supported by the narrative portion of the commission's report, the summary arguments that the report offers for the changes, or the scholarly literatures—on surprise attacks, on the principles of intelligence, on employees' incentives, psychology, and cognition, on organization and reorganization theory, and on the experiences of other nations—that, although highly pertinent, the commission's report ignores. On the contrary, those literatures, and the commission's own narrative of what went wrong before 9/11 in the response to the threat posed by al Qaeda, cast grave doubt on the soundness of its proposals.

The commission was impelled to make ambitious organizational recommendations by the desire to have something positive to show for its efforts besides a descriptive report (valuable as that would have been) and by a sense that the only recommendations that would make the requisite splash yet have a good chance of being adopted would be for an organizational overhaul. The existing organization of U.S. intelligence being a decentralized one, the proposal, if it was to be a proposal for change, *had* to be to centralize, even though centralization of intelligence is full of perils. Not necessarily more perils than those of a decentralized system, for within broad limits the performance of an intelligence system is insensitive to precisely how the system is organized. But the commission and Congress went too far. Concerns with the "pluralistic" character of the U.S. intelligence system that have merit could, as I have just suggested, have been addressed by separating the directorship of central intelligence from the directorship of the CIA and giving the DCI somewhat greater powers. But even if in the long run the structure that emerges from the act and its implementation will not be demonstrably worse than what we have now (it may not even be dramatically different from what we have now), the transition costs tip the balance against the act.

And probably the structure *will* be worse, unless the President is adroit in using the leeways created by the vagueness of the Reform Act to pull its sting. The layering of another official over the existing structure—the Director of National Intelligence, who is to be more than a mere board or committee chairman, who is to seize the reins and guide the horses but whose powers are ill-defined and overlap those of other powerful officials—is likely to engender constant conflict with the heads of the intelligence services, especially the CIA, and with the services' department heads, such as the Secretary of Defense and the Secretary of Homeland Security. The DNI may well find himself overloaded with duties that prevent him from performing the advisory and coordinating functions assigned him by the act, and embroiled in interagency conflict. The flow of information will be impeded and distorted by the lengthening of the bureaucratic distance between the operating level of the intelligence system and the policymaking level, at which responses to intelligence are devised. Intelligence may become more politicized than it is at present because of the concentration of power in one person whom the President can lean on to produce estimates that will support Presidential initiatives that may be bad policy though clever politics. And if the DNI does fulfill the legislative directive to bring about greater uniformity in the intelligence community, it may be at the price of retarding both the production of accurate intelligence data, and the imaginative analysis of the data, by reducing the diversity of organization cultures that fosters innovative thinking.

There is a possible way out, however, that can be seen by posing the choice facing the DNI as follows: it is between substance and management. The DNI can immerse himself in substantive intelligence issues, such as identifying and prioritizing the principal threats facing the United States and the intelligence strategies for meeting them; or he can try to manage the intelligence system better than it has been managed, with particular reference to the technical services. If he follows the former route, as he will have to do if he decides to assume responsibility for briefing the President, he will set himself up for a knock-down fight with the director of the CIA. If he follows the latter route, he will be conforming the role of the DNI to the role the Director of Central Intelligence might have played had the jobs of DCI and DCIA been separated.

The goal of the reorganization instituted by the Intelligence Reform Act is to prevent another surprise attack on the United

States. But the literatures reviewed in this book teach that surprise attacks are difficult to anticipate, at best, because of systemic, career, and cognitive characteristics of the intelligence
task that are extremely difficult to alter by structural (or, for
that matter, other) changes. Central is the asymmetry of
attacker and victim that makes it easy for the former to obtain
through surprise at least a local success—but he may be willing
to settle for that. The costs of false alarms are a key consideration as well, in helping to show why it can be entirely rational
for national security officials to refuse to heed signs of an
impending attack. There is also the paradox of the strength of
weakness. Surprise—the favored tactic of the weak adversary
because of its force-multiplying effect—is maximized by choosing a low-valued target and is likely to succeed because a
rational potential victim devotes only limited resources to trying to prevent a weak adversary's attack on such a target. In
short, the prevention of surprise attacks may pose problems
that even the best intelligence system could not overcome. Recognition of this fact is the beginning of realism in the redesign
of the system.

One of the cognitive limitations that impedes prevention of
surprise attacks and is particularly relevant to evaluating the
9/11 Commission's proposals and the congressional response
is the expectation that the future will repeat the past. Just as
generals prepare to fight the previous war, intelligence agencies and their critics prepare to prevent the previous surprise
attack. The commission's proposals are implicitly oriented
toward preventing a more or less exact repetition of the 9/11
attacks and other relatively low-tech attacks by Islamist terrorists. Yet they are among the least likely forms of a future terrorist attack because surprise has been lost. We give our
adversaries little credit if we suppose that the only attack they

can launch is the one we've anticipated. They didn't make that mistake on 9/11; why should they now?

The commission's report mentions only in passing the greater potential threat posed by weapons of mass destruction in the hands of terrorists or enemy states.[1] Deadly pathogens, lethal gases, and even small atomic bombs can be fabricated almost anywhere in the world and, because of their small size, delivered surreptitiously to the United States and activated by a small number of terrorists or foreign agents. A terrorist gang may even be able to buy an atomic bomb. We cannot seal our borders against such deliveries. Attacks with such weapons would be particularly difficult to anticipate because the range of possible targets is almost infinite and, in the case of biological terrorism, because the site of the attack need not even be in the United States. A lethal pathogen dispensed as an aerosol at almost any major airport in the world could cause a devastating worldwide epidemic. The attacker wouldn't have to pass through airport security and the airport wouldn't have to be in the United States even if this country was the intended target. The lethal pathogen most suitable for such an attack—the smallpox virus—is difficult to procure because all known specimens of the virus are locked up under tight security in a pair

1. See, for example, Graham Allison, *Nuclear Terrorism: The Ultimate Preventable Catastrophe* (2004); *The Gathering Biological Warfare Storm* (Jim A. Davis and Barry R. Schneider, eds., 2004); Richard A. Posner, *Catastrophe: Risk and Response* 71–86 (2004); *Grave New World: Security Challenges in the 21st Century*, chs. 1, 2, 4 (Michael E. Brown, ed., 2003); National Research Council of the National Academies, Committee on Science and Technology for Countering Terrorism, *Making the Nation Safer: The Role of Science and Technology in Countering Terrorism* (2002); Paul Schulte, "Intelligence and Weapons Proliferation in a Changing World," in *Agents for Change: Intelligence Services in the 21st Century* 203 (Harold Shukman, ed., 2000). For a recent warning, see Warren Rudman et al., "'Our Hair Is on Fire,'" *Wall Street Journal*, Dec. 16, 2004, p. A16.

of U.S. and Russian laboratories. But advances in biotechnology[2] may soon enable the virus to be synthesized.[3]

An active program of foreign intelligence of unprecedented scope and technological sophistication is needed—and more: a program that can anticipate technological surprises in the form of new, more lethal weapons of mass destruction or means of delivering them. To these issues the commission's report pays virtually no attention because they are so different from the issues presented by the 9/11 attacks themselves.

As far as one can judge from the report and other sources, the failure to prevent the 9/11 attacks, insofar as it should be regarded as culpable rather than as the unavoidable consequence of the inherent limitations of warning intelligence and of action in response to such intelligence, was managerial rather than organizational. The sole exception, given unaccountably short shrift by the 9/11 Commission and its congressional supporters (or for that matter opponents), may be the unhappy marriage of criminal investigation and domestic intelligence in the FBI, which hampered and continues to hamper the FBI's performance of the domestic intelligence function.

I ventured three modest suggestions for managerial reform in Chapter 4: increased investment in research on artificial intelligence that might assume more of the task of collecting and analyzing intelligence data; more generous early retirement benefits for intelligence officers to encourage greater analytic boldness; and opportunities for intelligence officers to be promoted to nonmanagerial positions. A fourth suggestion, which I have already mentioned, derives from the fact that while the creation of the DNI is now a done deal, his powers

2. See, for example, Jingdongl Tian et al., "Accurate Multiplex Gene Synthesis from Programmable DNA Microchips," 432 *Nature* 1050 (2004).

3. Nicholas Wade, "A DNA Success Raises Bioterror Concern," *New York Times* (late ed.), Jan. 12, 2005, p. A17.

remain to be defined by the President and by himself, and it is possible that, in practice, he will be more like a chairman of the board than, as the 9/11 Commission hoped, a CEO: more like the erstwhile Director of Central Intelligence, had that now defunct official been relieved of having to run the CIA as well, than like an intelligence "czar." He might then focus on improving coordination, especially at the design and planning stages, of the different technical systems for collecting intelligence data.

To managerial failure the standard and sensible and most important response is simply to change managers. The exit of George Tenet as head of the CIA has been seen in that light (possibly mistakenly). The erroneous assessment of Saddam Hussein's program of weapons of mass destruction was one intelligence failure too many, so now we have a new broom, sweeping vigorously,[4] though whether wisely or not, and with what effect, has yet to be seen; we shall have a second broom as soon as the President appoints the first Director of National Intelligence.

In a misguided quest for unanimity and a determination to use the political calendar and a public relations campaign to force precipitate action on weakly supported proposals for far-reaching organizational change, the 9/11 Commission, abetted by a stampeded Congress and a politically cornered President and a press that failed to subject the commission's recommendations to the searching scrutiny that the modern press reserves for scandals, disserved the cause of national security in a dangerous era. It did so by successfully promoting a bureaucratic reorganization that is more likely to be a recipe for bureaucratic infighting, impacted communication, dimin-

---

4. Douglas Jehl, "Director of Analysis at C.I.A. Is the Latest to Be Forced Out," *New York Times* (national ed.), Dec. 29, 2004, p. A1.

ished performance, tangled lines of command, and lowered morale than an improvement on the previous system.

It may, moreover, induce complacence about our "reformed" intelligence system and by doing so deflect attention from graver threats than a repetition of 9/11. If the public believes that the Intelligence Reform Act has fixed the system— if it believes that *any* reforms can ensure against intelligence failures—it will be less willing to support (and pay for) the strengthening of the other elements of an integrated system of national defense, including deterrence, border defense, and the guarding and hardening of potential targets. Such a relaxation of effort would be an invitation to disaster. If one conclusion emerges most strongly from this study, it is that warning intelligence has inherent limits that make it unrealistic to suppose that any intelligence system, no matter how configured, can guarantee the nation against being surprised by another, and perhaps far more devastating, attack.

Index